NO HANDICAP TO DANCE

NO HANDICAP TO DANCE

Creative Improvisation for People with and without Disabilities

GINA LEVETE

A CONDOR BOOK
SOUVENIR PRESS (E & A) LTD

ISBN 0 285 64966 3 (casebound)
ISBN 0 285 64961 2 (paperback)

Photoset and printed by
Photobooks (Bristol) Limited
Barton Manor, St Philips, Bristol

CONTENTS

INTRODUCTION

Although this book is dedicated to handicapped students, it is for everyone who finds pleasure in movement and in exploring the imagination.

The book is divided into three chapters. The first describes how I came to work with disabled students; the second is a practical guide suggesting ways and ideas for creative movement/improvisation sessions. These 'method classes' contain ideas which are simple to use if the reader has only a limited experience of dance and drama; equally they may be useful for dance teachers. All the suggested sessions have been given to able and disabled people alike. My approach has always been to regard either able or disabled students simply as 'students' and wherever possible I make no distinction in the content of the programme. However, it would be unrealistic not to recognise certain needs and so there are small sections with particular suggestions or points to remember for individual handicaps, as well as specific comments throughout this part of the book. I would recommend reading the whole of the dance section, as some of the suggestions and advice given, let us say, in the 3–6 year old section, may equally apply to adult students.

If you want to dance there is absolutely no reason to feel that because of a physical or mental limitation it is not possible to do so. Every human being is born with a sense of rhythm and movement within. This can be outwardly expressed through the eyes, the face, the head, the fingers, the feet – through any part of the body that is able to move. It is not possible to describe on paper the enjoyment that a movement session can bring to people who wanted to dance but hitherto had not realised that they could do so.

The third part of the book describes how my work with disabled students continued and developed into an organisation called Shape. Shape introduced many artists of different skills into creatively neglected pockets of the community, it enabled artists to widen their area of work and focused on the importance of everyone having the right to participate in the cultural life of the community. There is a growing awareness that participating in creative activities or entertainment, particularly outside isolated environments, such as institutions, hospitals and centres, can help to prevent social isolation and enable many more people to have an active community life. The aim of this last chapter is to describe the value of making use of many different arts activities. I would hope that those who read this account will be encouraged to introduce new creative projects. Very rarely is it possible to start with all the required assets, but if you want to do something it is usually possible to do it.

I should like to say thank you to Doctor Claus Newman, the Baring Foundation, the Carnegie United Kingdom Trust, the Gulbenkian Foundation and the Kings Fund Centre for making it possible to write up this work, to Charlotte Coudrille for the help she gave in correcting and typing the manuscript and to Ian Chapman for taking most of the photographs. Finally, thank you to all my friends in hospitals, prisons and centres, without whom I should not have had the opportunity and experience to recognise that there is no handicap to dance.

1: THE BEGINNING

Looking back on the past twelve years I realise how fortunate I am to have been in so many different surroundings where there is so much love.

It all began when my youngest child was running up a hill. Only five years old, she quickly overtook a boy in front who walked with enormous effort. 'Silly walks' were not even recognised then. The boy stopped and watched the small girl shoot past. He grinned at me and with difficulty said, 'She is better at it than me.' We talked. He told me that he was at a small private school 'for people like us.' That spastic boy was the spark that lit an idea.

For some time I had wanted to use my dance background in a new way. Now it seemed obvious how I might do this. When I dance it makes me feel good. The boy had loved the way that Sarah ran. There was the same sense of dance within him. Surely there must be many others unable to give outward expression to their inborn gift of movement and rhythm because society required their bodies and minds to perform in the same way as the majority of people.

The day after our meeting I went round to the school the boy had mentioned and asked to see the principal. The school was in a large Victorian house and was less like a school than any place could be. It was run by a round Dickensian-looking man called Mr Gubbins. Mr Gubbins cared for twelve young people who were well enough to travel to the school. Although it was a private establishment, the boys were sent through the local authority. It was an unusual situation, for the local authority would not in fact recognise the school because of Gubbins' unorthodox methods. If these methods had not been so unconventional, probably my work would never have begun.

Mr Gubbins laid great emphasis on encouraging people to be creative. He agreed to let me take dance sessions with his pupils, provided that I should work on his ideas too. Had I known beforehand what that would entail, I might have backed down. He was a great devotee of the classics. The boys were sent out with me in charge to make a film based on the Greek legend of Ariadne and the Golden Thread. Passers-by in Richmond Gardens stared in amazement as spastic, autistic and other young people dressed in bizarre homemade Greek clothes jumped about in the subway that linked the gardens to the river. I was both director and cameraman. At the same time I was trying desperately not to allow my colleagues or myself to be put off by the evident amusement of the accumulating crowd of onlookers. Worse was to come when, returning triumphantly to the school, Gubbins said, 'Now edit it.' I am sure this was the beginning of my love for theatre improvisation. Somehow the wobbly spastic fingers, the silent and sometimes frightening autistic boy and I managed to put together a film which in our opinion was nothing short of brilliant.

The next assignment was to produce an end of term play for the parents, based on the story of the death of Socrates. I apologetically said that I was not familiar with the works of Plato. Gubbins plied me with books. The role of Socrates was played by a student whose obsession was train timetables and time in general. His daily greeting was, 'What time does your watch make it? Did you take the train from Waterloo, or one on another line?' His performance as Socrates was very real until it came to the end of the death scene. He could wait no longer and began to punctuate the dying moments with time checks.

These were happy days. It was my introduction to people with recognised abnormalities. It was my introduction to a caring, loving situation in which both principal and pupils had a sense of innocence. If it seemed that they were only 'playing', at least the result was one of stimulus and vitality. Many more orthodox centres that I have encountered since then do not possess the spontaneity of Mr Gubbins' school. Yet this genial man was constantly rebuffed by local education authorities. He did not fit for size. The mad are allowed to be eccentric but the sane eccentric is always regarded with suspicion.

In our endeavour to make life tolerable for the disabled, care must be taken not to obliterate the individual personality. It is only too easy to create a bright airy classroom with all the right equipment and teachers with recognised training. Yet the room needs character and warmth before the real light will come in.

Having seen the response to the dance sessions at the school, I felt it was time to move on and to concentrate on introducing dance movement to a wider range of the disabled. I approached the Inner London Education Authority Special Schools Department and offered my services, with little result. Although I had had a four-year specialised dance training and was a member of the Imperial Society of Teachers of Dance, this was not accepted as sufficient qualification. It looked as if the only way to get in was to find a particular school interested in having such classes.

After a search I met the principal of a special school for physically handicapped children. Miss Mathews was herself physically disabled. She listened to my proposal and then pointed out the enormous and varying degrees of handicap in her charges. These included cases of spina bifida, heart problems, spasticity, muscular dystrophy, hydrocephalus and other disorders. Why did I think I could use dance movement with such disabilities, having no real experience or medical background? I explained that the way I worked was to regard the students as just another group of children, similar to the children who came to the children's theatre where I was at this time giving improvisation classes. My feeling was that Miss Mathews' pupils must adapt their disabilities to the session, rather than the other way about. If I identified with each handicap, the spontaneity and magic would be lost for them.

This small woman who cared so much for the welfare of her pupils looked at me long and hard. 'All right,' she said. 'Find a pianist. I want you to work with a pianist. We will try.' I returned to the education authority equipped with a willing primary school. It was agreed that there should be a trial of two terms, two afternoons a week. I cannot remember how Stuart, the pianist, and I encountered each other. He was a young composer who, in order to survive musically, sold insurance at the weekends.

We arrived for our first afternoon. The physiotherapists had agreed to mention any movements that a child should not do. For example, those with certain heart problems should not be asked to raise their arms high. Otherwise it was decided that the children should take the responsibility themselves for how much they could do.

I looked at these young and desperately physically handicapped children. Stuart looked at me as if to say, 'Go on, you said you could.' A small blond boy of eight or nine, who looked as if a puff of wind would blow him away, said from his chair in an excited voice, 'Miss Mathews said we are going to dance. Can we?' 'We certainly are,' I replied, 'we are going to do just about everything.' We asked the physiotherapists if everyone who was able could lie or sit on the floor. Others had to remain in their chairs. All the children began to dance with whatever movement they had – their faces, their eyes, fingers, half a body, a whole body – it did not matter with how much or how little. I discovered that if I told a story and Stuart came in with the music after a few sentences, they would dance and act better because the words gave them time to gather together the little movement they had. One such story was based on head circling and turning movements for the children who could only use their heads and maybe a weak hand. A story would go as follows:

Mary sat in her chair looking sad.
　(*Music*)
In front of her was a round plate of spaghetti.
　(*Music*)
She shook her head and peered forward.
'What is on the plate?' she asked.
She turned her head one way.
Then she turned her head the other way.
She looked up.
She looked down.
She looked cross.
　(*Music*)
A man came bouncing in, carrying a box full of spectacles.
'What you need is glasses,' he said.
　(*Music*)
He took out a pair and put them on her.

Too loose.
Another.
Too tight.
Mary twisted her face, wrinkled her nose and shut her eyes.
    (*Music*)
'Try these.' The man put another pair on her.
Mary opened her eyes.
She looked up.
She looked to the side,
and to the other side.
She looked down.
'Oh,' she squealed, 'spaghetti! My favourite food!'
She twisted the fork around the spaghetti.
She lifted her head and dropped the spaghetti into her mouth.
    (*Music*)
She rubbed her tummy.
DELICIOUS!

Each session began with some formal exercises, then a movement game that enabled the children to travel. How many things can you touch that feel cold? How many things can you touch before the music stops? Each session concentrated on one or two movements. Therefore, if the session was based on touch, the next stage was an improvisation of their own concerning contact, usually moving in whatever way they wished to Stuart's music. It is important when planning sessions for physically handicapped children that a class has a structure that introduces ideas and improves the quality of movement, while at the same time allowing the children freedom to make use of their own movement potential. Pupils should experiment with perhaps one or two ideas in every possible way during a session. There can be no right or wrong technique, for it is the interpretation and capability of the individual that counts. One rule I made was that whatever they did must never be dull for the onlooker; therefore timing and originality were qualities to be developed. When giving a class, it is necessary to be flexible and sensitive in your timing to adapt to their ability to concentrate. If a session is prepared that the children seem unable to respond to, it is better to switch to another track and to use that programme at another time.

By the time the trial two terms were up the children had made much progress, learning to create compositions with their fertile imagination and discovering many ways of moving. Most important of all, they had had fun. An inspector came to watch a session. She liked what she saw but said that unless I was prepared to do a teacher training course (two years) I could only remain until the end of the year.

On the last afternoon the physiotherapists greeted me with welcome and surprising news. They felt that dance movement with the children had been beneficial and they were annoyed that a relatively new idea should cease. On their own initiative they had organised an interview for me with two medical consultants at Queen Mary's Hospital, Roehampton. The consultants were in charge of a unit that looked after the physically handicapped children who came for artificial limb fittings and training in how to use them. They had a special interest in the very young thalidomide people and spina bifida cases. Both consultants immediately responded to the idea. The problem was, as always, who should pay me? I said that I was prepared to work voluntarily for three months, until it had been established that the work was valuable. I was asked what I hoped the children would achieve from my particular approach. 'Fun,' I replied. They seemed relieved at the answer. "Thank goodness for no scientific explanation," said the consultant. He was at that time in the process of handing over the unit to Doctor Claus Newman. This busy man has always found time since then to encourage and supervise all that has evolved from this small beginning.

I worked with the thalidomide and spina bifida children for six years. After the first few months, the Lady Hoare Trust* sponsored the classes. I earned five pounds a week. Children who had simply a trunk with small flippers were incredibly agile. Their imagination and personalities were very exciting to

*Lady Hoare as Lord Mayoress of London launched the Thalidomide Appeal and retained an active and effective interest in the welfare of children for the rest of her life.

work with. It was an outlet they needed, to have classes which enabled them to enact any situation they might have wished to be in had it not been for their handicap. The improvisation sessions at Queen Mary's were almost identical to the ones I gave at the children's theatre, the only difference being that there was more emphasis on exercises and games that allowed and encouraged them to socialise and have physical contact with each other.

Their various degrees of handicap often made them elitist in their attitude towards each other. 'I'm not going to be his partner because he hasn't got legs,' was a remark made by a child with legs but with only one arm. At the time it shocked me, although on reflection it was no different from the labels we all use every day. To help them work better together, part of each class was devoted to making them adapt to each other's physical limitations. They enjoyed movement games, such as forming the letters of the alphabet, numbers or words with their bodies. 'Terry can't make "A" with us, he hasn't got arms or legs,' one of them would say. Terry retorted, 'Don't be stupid. I can be the bar that goes across.' They became incredibly quick at building shapes together. This developed later into improvising with words and composing short plays.

The spina bifida children were far more timid. They needed a lot of encouragement to get out of their 'Chailey Chariots' which are like go-carts. Once out, they shunted around on their bottoms or stomachs with joy. When very young, they have difficulty in recognising the feel of different surfaces. So again tactile movements were introduced. "Can you put your forehead against a surface that is cold?" I would ask. 'Put your back against something soft. Touch everyone in the room who has curly hair." And so forth. Great care was needed to ensure that their brittle little bones did not fracture because, due to their paralysis, they would not feel the break. Despite this, they quickly grew to be adventurous, discovering different movement combinations for travelling across the room. All the children under the age of 12–14 preferred to be without artificial limbs or calipers. Everyone from parents to staff agreed that the classes were successful in 'thawing out' these small people who came into the hospital. It was not possible to measure the success of dance in improving their wellbeing. It *was* possible to assess the benefits. These were enjoyment, stimulus, discovery of movement potential, losing their shyness with each other and learning to express themselves articulately.

After a time, I felt mine would also be helpful. I applied for and was fortunate to be given a Churchill Fellowship. This was an everyman's opportunity award, and a superb concept. It did not matter if you had no academic or specialised training. If you had an idea that could benefit your craft as well as the community and you could learn more by travelling abroad, these scholarships were for such a purpose. I was allowed to go to Paris for three months to develop my rudimentary knowledge of mime and theatre improvisation. At the same time I was able to visit French hospitals to see if similar work was being done.

The three months put me on a new path. I found a gifted teacher who had worked with Marceau and then formed his own technique in improvisation. The introduction to this course was unusual for me, having only experienced a formal ballet training. Six of us on the course were told to go out into the courtyard and feel our surroundings. For the first few seconds I thought this was rubbish. We should at least be 'doing' something. Then, out of necessity to 'do' something, I looked at the blades of grass between the cobblestones. I listened to the silence. I began to feel, not think, and started to slow down. After ten minutes we were called back to stand in the studio and recapture the experience of the courtyard. From then onwards the work was fascinating, challenging and technically quite difficult.

Alongside the course, I visited a number of French hospitals and institutions and spoke in broken French with many staff about using professional artists in situations of disability. At that time in France not much was happening. Serious interest was expressed. I was invited to take a session at one hospital. The children had a miserable time because of my disastrous French. Having told them to lie down, I could not remember the words for 'stand up'.

During this period of scholarship I realised how necessary it is for everyone to 'recharge' from time to time. Being a student again, at whatever age, allows a sense of freedom and opportunity.

On returning to Queen Mary's, I decided somehow to find funds that would allow me to work with two other artists. We should try to offer our services to every kind of patient, but as a result of changed personal circumstances, if I was to continue in this direction it was necessary to have a small salary. Applying for a grant was my first introduction to the painful task of fund raising. I had no contacts and at that time knew nothing about relevant foundations or trusts. Finding the right person to write to was like tracing the right path in a maze. At this time the idea of the performing arts being used to play a healing role was virtually unheard of. Then a door opened. The Leverhulme Trust, after a thorough investigation of the proposal, gave Westminster Hospital Special Trustees on my behalf £20,000 to be divided into four yearly instalments of £5,000 as a research grant. I advertised for two people interested in working part-time on this project. Ian, a visual artist who lectured at an art school, and Richard, a free-lance photographer, and myself formed a team which was to be the lead for Shape. I worked full time and I realised in the early stages of the project that if we were to make an impact with our work it was essential to have good secretarial backing. Julie, who had worked as a secretary to a director of Shell and now had two small babies, was glad to help us. She really was the lynch-pin in the project. She worked one and a half days a week from her home. She made the task of being an innovator less lonely, as I had somehow I could bounce ideas onto.

The first priority was to establish what creative activities were happening already in hospitals throughout the United Kingdom. The undertaking was enormous for two people but, amidst babies crawling over the floor and orange juice in unbreakable non-spill plastic cups, we managed to circulate about 2,680 hospitals. The returned questionnaires showed that little use was being made of the arts. With this information we were encouraged to spread out as far as possible and offer our skills to many areas of social disadvantage. Richard, the photographer, was teaching limbless children to use polaroid cameras and make compositions. Ian, the visual artist, was experimenting with silk-screen printing and batik for severely handicapped adults. I was using dance with psychiatric patients, old people, stroke patients and prison inmates. At the same time, it was most important not to lose contact with our work outside these areas. I took part in many classes for different forms of dance, mime and acting so that I could see other people's ideas and not lose the focus on quality. There is a danger of people becoming so enthusiastic about working with these new groups that they wish to devote all their time to the work. This is fatal. They are not trained social or medical workers and consequently the situation will drain them if there is no balance. The students will suffer because the quality will drop. If a proper perspective is kept, both sides gain. The artist adds an extra dimension to his work from having contact with people who through their suffering have enormous appreciation and awareness and whose surroundings are full of caring people. Sometimes when I had finished working in a hospital, coming back into the outside world could be a cold experience. Often I wondered why the same care with each other was not taken in everyday living. People are fragile, we all so easily and repeatedly break each other's confidence.

The three of us gave mixed media workshops at weekends. These were open to anyone but they were arranged particularly for staff in the caring professions to give them ideas they might be able to use with their own students. There was a combination of dance and visual art or drama and photography; sometimes we even put three forms together. The workshops were very useful to students who often started out the day nervously, but by the end of a morning session were relaxed, exploding with ideas, and having fun. Working with staff to show what we were doing was as important as working with the patients. Therefore the next step was to persuade principals at teaching hospitals to allow a time within a medical student's already very full programme for such activities. Eventually the School of Physiotherapy at St Mary's Hospital, Paddington, agreed to an eight-week course in dance and theatre improvisation.

Once one hospital had said 'yes', a number of others followed suit. These students were surprisingly difficult to work with at first. Their rigid training did not allow for what seemed to them frivolity. It was only after a tentative and suspicious start that the students began to understand the connection between their own skills and the approach of the artist. The emphasis of the classes was to help them project themselves in a manner that would encourage the patient to gain confidence. I felt the medical students should first play the role of the patient, so that they could try to imagine and understand their fears and doubts and their need for confidence. Such 'projection' need not be regarded as having to 'act' but, used truthfully and with the right energy, can become a life force that helps physiotherapists and occupational therapists to heal. Many of the students took up dance as a hobby after the course was over. Nowadays more hospitals are aware how such theatre work can complement a training programme, and Woolfgang Stange, a young German dancer, has carried on the original courses with other medical students.

The thalidomide children were by now adolescents. They required a different kind of session. Many of them were very conscious of their deformities, and were reticent about getting out of their chairs. A number were rather aggressive. It seemed necessary to structure acting sessions that would give them a sense of purpose. Therefore we improvised plays and stories which were taped for other ill children to listen to in bed. Their imaginations were so fertile that it was no problem to find a story line, but a structure was still needed on which to base the play. I would give them a cue. For example, I would turn on the school room tap to create a sound of running water as an opening for the play. They picked up from there, made their own sound effects and improvised the dialogue until satisfied with the results. We then taped the story.

The teenage girls liked exercises that kept them in good shape. By now students often took the class themselves, making up their own exercises for each other. Since theirs was the experience of being in wheelchairs they knew exactly what exercises were required. Music was important and had to be up to the minute.

Susan, who had been with me since the age of four, wanted to know if I thought she could learn to teach movement. She had no limbs and used to give sessions for the young children by holding a drum with her flippers and putting the drumstick in her mouth. She had had an inborn sense of movement from the outset. I received her question with mixed emotions. I was worried that if I advised her not to do this, she would become more disheartened with her own disability, but I was absolutely delighted that, recognising her handicap, she saw no reason not to ask for advice in pursuing such a career. I told her that dance teaching was an over-subscribed profession and she and her parents should consider whether it was worth the risk of embarking on a dance course. Later Susan decided to train as a telephonist. She is now happily married.

I wondered at first whether the elderly people with whom I was working would feel insulted at the suggestion of dance exercise. The answer was no. Provided it was explained to them how dance could help their wellbeing, they were most anxious to take part. Any method which would contribute to keeping their bodies active was welcome. I enjoyed so much working with such appreciative, humorous and wise people. In the second chapter of this book there are details of movement classes for the elderly.

Short-stay psychiatric patients needed a very different approach. They divided themselves into two sections, those who were withdrawn and preferred to work alone in class, and those who were anxious to share their experiences with the whole group. These people were more than likely to return to the mainstream of society. Holding their concentration could be difficult, partly because of the prescribed drugs, partly due to their private fears and suspicions. I based most classes around the idea of encouraging students to 'let go'. 'Letting go' in no way meant being out of control. Dance is a tremendous outlet in such situations. I learned much from these students, who were so sensitive as a group to any of their colleagues' sudden and irrational behaviour. People who have undergone the awful experience of a nervous breakdown often grow in tolerance and sensitivity, which equips them better to understand human behaviour. Trying to persuade the nursing staff to join in was important. They found it difficult to participate, probably because the role of staff/patient puts up an unconscious barrier. When they did take part the patients were delighted. It is important when working with psychiatric patients to ensure that movements are relaxed and that adequate time is allowed for breathing exercises. The pace of the class should be adapted to the energy of the students on a particular day. Enough time should be allowed afterwards to stay and talk. This is all part of a good workshop.

On a visit to psychiatric hospitals in New York I investigated the training for becoming a dance therapist. I watched and took part in dance therapy sessions at Wards Island and the Bronx Psychiatric Hospitals. The training in the USA is very sound. No one may enrol to do the therapy training without having had a full professional dance background and a period of time performing. In the United Kingdom at present we do not have an adequate similar course. Until such time as we do, it would be better not to lay claims that 'dance therapists' are properly trained in the United Kingdom. The therapy sessions I took part in were run almost as a disco dance. The whole hour might look too casual to an observer, but in fact the sessions were beautifully structured to fit contemporary social requirements. Throughout, there was a subtle emphasis on incorporating many elements of a therapist's approach aimed towards bringing people out of themselves.

Giving dance sessions at Holloway Prison was yet another experience. On my first visit I was asked to work in a room where a number of other activities were all taking place at the same time. The women had not had movement classes before. I wandered around rather forlornly trying to find customers. 'Would you like to try out some dance exercises; it helps to tone up the body?' Retorts hurtled back, such as, 'You must be joking, who are we toning up for?' 'With the diet here, love, it's a losing battle.'' ''Is it good for my sex life?'' The women were amused. I played some music and started warming up by myself. A large black woman, who had been staring at me for a time, came up, cupped my chin in her hand and looked straight into my eyes. She said, 'I read you very clear. You is walking in a jungle on the outside, we is in a jungle here.' She was right. At that time I had a number of personal problems. From then on the women completely accepted me. I so enjoyed being with them. In such situations people are just themselves, they either accept you or not. It was far less hypocritical than many outside encounters. I would never have presumed to enquire why they were there, but often they wished to talk. So many strange sad stories were explained. The opportunity of knowing these women is one I cherish.

Using dance for stroke patients was done with the purpose of helping to co-ordinate movement and to stimulate memory by performing a sequence of movements. These students needed more energy and encouragement than those at any of the other places I worked. They were so easily depressed, and had to make a great effort to draw on inner reserves of courage and will themselves to improve their condition. Many times I left the hospital drained, wondering if the past hour had helped at all. It is so important to understand intuitively yet not to identify with any of the problems or illnesses. If you do begin to identify yourself with them, then it is sensible to take a break and begin to work again when you can distance yourself from the patient.

During these four years I often felt very much alone. It was a time when we were continually trying to persuade new groups to make use of the team. We did not belong anywhere. We arrived, took a session, and left. Sometimes someone had forgotten to get patients ready; at other times patients were not available because of another activity. I made many fruitless journeys. The continuity of a group was never stable because, happily, patients get better. This irregularity meant presenting a class to some people for the first time, while at the same session developing the content for the regulars. Long stay hospitals and day centres were easier in this respect.

The work was just beginning to be heard about by a number of arts organisations and voluntary groups. I was invited to give talks, often without even repayment of expenses. I would arrive to find an audience of three people. Again there would be apologies as someone had forgotten to tell the staff. I knew that, however annoyed I was, I must offer to return. It was essential to explain the concept of our work. Often I told myself that when the four years came to an end I would change back. But nature always compensated for these moments of exhaustion and gloom. The next workshop would prove such fun for the patients and for myself that it prompted yet another new area. Those four years proved to be just preparation for the organisation of a much wider venture – Shape.

In the next chapter I shall describe in detail ways in which dance improvisation can be used. All workshops written about have been given to able and disabled people and show that there really need not be a handicap to dance.

2: PRACTICAL GUIDE TO CREATIVE MOVEMENT WORKSHOPS

This chapter outlines frameworks within which many of your own or the suggested ideas can be introduced. The ideas can easily be used by those who have a limited dance or drama experience, as well as by professional dancers and teachers of dance.

What is Improvisation?

Before embarking on a movement improvisation class it is necessary to examine the word improvisation. It is something most of us have to do every day of our lives. We try to make the most suitable composition out of situations that face us, almost from the time we are born. When a baby discovers it can move, he or she experiments with ways of getting across the room. All human beings are creative in some way. Professional artists do not have a monopoly of 'creativity'. Many people whose creative talents do not lie within the area of the arts may still enjoy participating in music, dance, visual art, writing and drama activities. They may wish to have the experience and 'feel' rather than to learn a technique. Improvisation workshops can allow these students freedom to explore their own potential in whatever direction they choose to channel it. For the student who is training to become a professional dancer, mastering a technique of dance is of primary importance. In this instance improvisation is not enough in itself, but is still an essential part of the student's syllabus. Improvisation is a wonderful outlet for expression and a creative game for the imagination.

Suggestions for the Tutor

1. It is important to bear in mind that when using this approach you are not 'teaching', but simply 'working with'

your group. Think of the words 'creative movement' rather than 'dance' for giving sessions such as I describe.

2.   The framework or structure of a session is to allow the individual's maximum potential to be drawn out, through movements, words and abstract ideas.

3.   It is important to plan a programme in advance and whenever possible to learn it by heart, but also to have notes at hand.

4.   Choice of music and sounds are very important. Choose and tape all music beforehand so that there is no fiddling about during the class trying to find the right track or part of the tape. Particularly with patients, this can sap their concentration and confidence. A drum and percussion instruments are necessary. Each programme should have time devoted to students working without accompanying sounds so that they can discover their own rhythm centres. It is not possible to suggest music as this has to be the tutor's individual choice. It is essential that you like the music and feel it interprets the ideas you wish to put across.

5.   Clear demonstration must always be given and clear examples when suggesting abstract ideas (see Method Classes).

6.   Flexibility to change a planned programme, if for some reason students do not respond well, is essential.

7.   Flexibility with regard to timing is also necessary. If students are tired, finish before the planned time. You will probably achieve a better result than if you rigidly adhere to your planned programme.

8.   Only ever plan a session that you enjoy yourself.

9.   Remember that first and foremost you are there to encourage people to have fun and extend themselves through this experience.

Suggestions on How to Make Use of the Guide

1.   I would suggest that the reader take ideas and themes from the Method Classes and then put them within their own framework, so that they have the stamp of their own personality. Again, I would stress the need to be at ease with a planned programme.

2.   Most classes when first planned on paper will contain too many ideas for one session and will need pruning. Very soon

you will recognise your own timing and a class will flow without having to time each part.

3.   Ideas from the adult section can be used with most groups of people over the age of 14, other than the elderly and stroke patients and, in some cases, the mentally disabled.

4.   There are few separate sections for different disabilities. In all sections there are comments and observations from sessions that I have given to handicapped students, and therefore it is important to read this whole chapter.

5.   There are suggestions for psychiatric patients, mentally disabled people and the visually impaired which contain examples of frameworks within which any of the general ideas can be introduced.

There are detailed descriptions of simple breathing exercises and exercises for the elderly.

This book is essentially to suggest ideas and structures rather than give detailed descriptions of how to move. I hope it will be of value to the reader. All the workshops written down have been given to widely differing people – prison inmates, the elderly, the mentally handicapped, the blind, psychiatric patients, the homeless, professional dancers, actors, physically able and disabled young people, housewives, business people, teachers, medical students and staff in the caring professions – all of whom wished to experience creative movement in some form.

Simple Breathing Exercises
To be used in part or as a whole with all Method Classes

STAGE 1

Sitting either in a chair or on the floor. The body in a relaxed upright position. Arms relaxed by sides if sitting on a chair, resting on crossover 'crossed leg' position if on the floor. Whenever possible work from a floor position.

1.   Take in a deep breath through the nostrils, feeling as if the stomach is filling up. The stomach extends like a piece of elastic on the inhalation. Four counts.

2.   Hold the breath for four counts.

3.   Exhale slowly through the nostrils. The stomach empties

and therefore contracts inwards. Feel that the last of the air is almost coming out at the base of the spine. Four counts.
4.   Hold empty for four counts.
Repeat three times. Describe the stomach action as like a pair of bellows: in, out, in, out.

STAGE 2
1.   Block the right nostril with the right forefinger. Breathe in as in Stage 1.
2.   Hold breath, but change nostrils and block the left nostril with the left forefinger. Four counts.
3.   Exhale, still holding left nostril shut (stomach action the same as in Stage 1).
4.   Hold. Four counts.
Repeat. Inhale, still holding left nostril shut. Then, while holding breath, change over to shut the right nostril. Exhale. Repeat three times.

STAGE 3
1.   Take in a deep breath through nostrils (stomach action: extension). Four counts.
2.   Sharply exhale through nostrils (stomach action: like bellows working fast or a piece of elastic – out, in, out, in – pushing the air out, in quick short bursts until all the air inhaled has been exhaled. It may be that at first you can only 'pump' out the air in 10–14 short bursts. Later as you breathe in more deeply you may manage more. After this stage take a deep breath in and exhale as Stage 1.
(This stage is strong and should not be repeated too often or students may feel giddy, though it is an excellent way of clearing the head. Perform Stage 3 only two or three times at first, and always Stage 1 in between each time.
   In all stages the body should remain upright, relaxed and still, no shoulders hunching, no strain across the chest. The only physical movement is the stomach going in and out.
   When I mention 'gentle breathing' or 'simple breathing' in the Method Classes, I am referring to Stage 1.

Suggestions for a Relaxation Talk-Through
Sometimes at the end of a creative movement session an

imagery 'talk-through' can help the body to relax. Each tutor can devise his or her own. These are examples of some that I use. I usually quietly tap the wood of the drum with a stick whilst speaking. Listening to some classical music can also be relaxing, but often a voice can be more effective.

RELAXATION TALK-THROUGH (1)

Lie flat on the floor with your eyes closed. Imagine you are lying on the beach. The sand is warm, the sun is shining down, the waves are lapping the store. Someone is very gently pouring warm sand over you, it trickles onto your face, your cheek, your neck, the warm sand runs down the back of your neck, your shoulders, the fronts of your arms. You feel so relaxed, the backs of your arms against the warm sand. The sand is pouring over your chest and stomach, down your back, your buttocks, down the fronts of your legs, your calves, your ankles, your feet, the soles of your feet. You are lying there absolutely relaxed, the sun warming you, just lying and feeling your mind at rest.

RELAXATION TALK-THROUGH (2)

Lie and breathe deeply. Lie on your back, feet about 30 cm apart, arms at sides, palms upwards. Close your eyes, breathe in for four counts, hold and out for four counts. In and out. Concentrate on your breath and let all thoughts dissolve, all the problems and tensions of the day are not important during this time of relaxation. Now relax your toes, let go of your feet, your ankles, calves, knees, back of the knees, thighs. Let go of your buttocks, your stomach. Relax your chest, your diaphragm, your spine. Let go of the back of your neck, relax your face, the cheeks, mouth, forehead, top of the head. Relax your eyes, your brain, let it rest, rest your heart, your stomach. Just rest. Lie and rest.

Let students lie peacefully for 3–10 minutes. If you notice someone is tense, then gently touch them wherever the tension is. Often gentle handling will allow psychiatric patients to have the confidence to let go. After deep relaxation ask students to come to a sitting position and breathe gently, opening eyes slowly, have a good stretch and then stand up when they are ready. Allow students to roll onto their sides before they stand up. This will prevent any giddiness.

RELAXATION TALK-THROUGH (3)
Lie flat on the floor. Shut your eyes and breathe gently. Feel that you are lying on a pink cloud, the cloud is soft and you rest your whole body in this pink fluffy cloud. You let each part of your body just sink into the cloud. No part of your body needs to work, the cloud just supports you. All your worries and tensions disappear through the cloud. This is the time for you to let yourself be empty. Just lie there gently floating, breathe gently, up and down, in and out, up and down, in and out. Let your hands and your fingers relax, your feet and toes, the back of your neck, chest, your buttocks, your stomach. The knees, back of knees, legs. Just float. Listen to silence, become part of silence.

WORKSHOPS FOR ABLE OR PHYSICALLY DISABLED CHILDREN

CHILDREN'S MOVEMENT IMPROVISATION (3–6 year olds)

Introduction
The following classes were given to both able-bodied and physically handicapped children. The physically handicapped children I worked with had widely differing handicaps, including many of the thalidomide victims who at the start of my work were aged about three or four years old. Many of these young people continued to take part in creative movement improvisation sessions until the age of 17 or 18. Some children were limbless, others partially paralysed, and others less disabled. They were of average intelligence, as a whole. Although these ideas can be used for any group of 3–6 year olds, my suggestions and comments are directed towards those working with the physically disabled. These classes are suitable for mentally disabled young people as well.

Whenever possible the children preferred to discard their

calipers, artificial limbs or wheelchairs. Those who were severely handicapped, unable to sit up, lay on rubber mats. The others sat on the floor. Those who had to remain in wheelchairs formed the rest of the circle. Always begin a session in a circle whenever possible.

If parents will come in and watch it is a good idea, as much of the sessions are games playing with movement. Parents who did attend often continued the games at home. On the other hand, for many parents it is a chance to go and have a cup of tea in peace. Therefore I would suggest that parents are made to feel welcome, but not obliged to watch. For this age group I prefer not to have adults join in. If children are totally involved in a session they are unaware of onlookers. Often students would sit in, and the group was not in the least inhibited.

The Structure of such sessions should start with formal direction and build to a climax that allows a child to use movements in his own way. With the very young, emphasis on a particular movement during an hour session is important, but unlike classes for older people it cannot be the 'theme' for the whole period of time.

Music: Choosing the right music can enhance the vitality of the children. Bear in mind that they listen to the radio and that reggae, disco, funk, ethnic music with a strong beat are sounds they grow up with. Part of a session should contain classical music as well. Electronic sounds are exciting for improvisation sequences. A drum will cost about four or five pounds and is invaluable. Percussion instruments for the children to use are also necessary. Maracas, tambours, wooden sticks, triangles, bells, wooden xylophones, are ideal. If these are not available the tutor could suggest to the classroom teacher that the children make homemade instruments during a craft or art session. Tins or yogurt cartons full of dried peas will do as shakers, sticks from a wood or garden, painted tins or wooden boxes to bang on. Proper instruments can be obtained from educational suppliers or shops. Wooden boxes of different sizes and shapes are very useful. Perhaps the hospital technicians could help, or a maintenance worker.

Size of Class: It is impossible to suggest the ideal number of students for a session. It depends on the circumstances. For the

3–6 age group, six to eight is a good number if they are physically or mentally disabled.

Space: The larger the space the more fun the class will be. A classroom with chairs and tables pushed back which has a large area is fine. A hospital ward with a large central space is also suitable. However it is very important not to expect children to move in a cramped space. It is the responsibility of the tutor to ensure that there is adequate space.

Special Suggestions for a Physically Disabled Children's Session

Some children may be mobile, others not. Almost certainly the group will have very varying degrees of handicap. Do not worry. Each child will work within his or her own limitations. Encourage those with artificial limbs to discard them (with staff approval, of course). At this age children generally prefer to move without them. Have rubber or foam mats for the severely disabled to lie on. Make sure children who have to remain in wheelchairs are spaced out between the more able bodied. To begin the class sit in a circle on the floor. The tutor *must* wear suitable flexible clothing. It is *essential* to demonstrate all the movements you expect the children to perform. Tight jeans or trousers are useless. Track suits, dance tights, loose lightweight trousers, are all ideal. The tutor will need to move around and demonstrate individually to severely handicapped pupils lying on mats. He or she will show how they can utilise and improvise with the movements they possess. Do not feel inhibited at referring to their different physical limitations. For example: 'Peter, you can only rock from side to side or move on your side, so this exercise will be more difficult for you. Do it how you want, but you could for example do it like this . . .' (Tutor demonstrates) Sometimes allow the children to perform a direction individually. Then point out to the others how they utilised the movement. For example: 'Mary could not use her arms for that, but it did not matter because her legs moved so excitingly and created the same shape.' Never talk down to any pupils and remember that there is more of a tendency to do this with disabled students. Give plenty of encouragement, but never settle for second best. You are there to help improve the quality of movement as well as to encourage creative ideas. If you feel the movement could be better, say so. I have two rules with all students of whatever age. Firstly, movements must be interesting to watch, and secondly, demonstration by a pupil must not go on too long so that it becomes boring and the group loses its concentration. With older groups, whatever emotional fantasy is being expressed, students must be able to 'cut' and return to themselves immediately because they are in complete control of their expression.

Encourage pupils to improvise with as many different ways of moving as is possible so that they discover their movement potential. Do not be afraid because the class is physically handicapped. You are not teaching them how to move, you are asking them to discover their own ways of moving, and instinctively these young people know their own limitations. Always talk to the staff before the class and always have at least one or two members of the nursing or school staff in the room, not, at this age, to join in, but to be there in case a child needs to go to the lavatory or needs help in some way.

NEVER physically 'place' a child in any position. You do not have the medical knowledge. Simply demonstrate the movements you wish them to do. Apart from the introductory exercises this is a class for their own ideas and discovery. However the introductory exercises in the 3–6 workshops will give a foundation for the quality of movement. What you can do is ensure that the quality of the stretch is really a 'stretch', not a halfway one where the fingers or legs are not fully extended. The only group of students who may need to be placed in certain exercises are the visually handicapped.

Suggestions for Mentally Disabled Students
The age range of pupils will be older in some instances, but they will still be content to take part in suggested sessions for 3–6 year olds.

Demonstrate very clearly. Develop a good control and quality of movement from the outset. The time to work on this is at an early age when students are first introduced to dance. If you can, introduce a wider vocabulary of movement, for example, spin, stretch flat, light, heavy, sharp, flowing, etc. By the time they reach the next stage they will possess a good standard of movement. From the outset make sure they are given the opportunity to improvise and experiment and think for themselves. Too often dance sessions for these children are just repetition of the tutor's movements.

Ideas that can be developed through the use of props (see suggestions on page 41) are important: how to go shopping, to the laundromat, get on the bus or tube, use the telephone. Acted out in a story form these are useful, particularly to institutionalised children.

A detailed description of formal exercises is given in the Method Class for this age group. *These exercises probably only take up 15 minutes of a session.* The tutor should demonstrate the exercises alongside the children, at least until they are acquainted with them. The Method Class contains too many ideas for a one-hour session – it is meant to be pruned.

Students of all ages should have at least one session a week. For older groups of mentally disabled students, twice a week is ideal. If movement is included at an early age as a serious part of their educational programme, by the time they have reached the age of ten or twelve those who still show interest in such classes will have a good foundation on which to extend their imaginations and movement potential.

Method Class for Children Aged 3–6
It is important to read the introductory suggestions on the previous pages before taking ideas from this class. The tutor demonstrates *all* directions. Sit in a large circle on the floor. Remember, take only a few of the ideas for your programme.
Content of Class: Movement exercises; travelling movement games; mime and dialogue; a group improvisation story which includes previous movements used; free improvisation; 'theme' movement; 'circling'.
Time: 1 hour
Purpose: Enjoyment, stimulus, discovery of movement potential, 'thawing out' (for hospitalised children).
Equipment: Tape recorder or record player; drum; percussion instruments.

1. FORMAL EXERCISES
Begin each session with simple exercises to strengthen and tone up the body. Each exercise should be repeated three times. Use

a drum to accompany directions and demonstration. Sit the group in a circle on the floor where possible.

Head Exercises

a.   Lift chin to ceiling. Drop chin to chest. Lift chin to central position.

b.   Turn now towards one side of the room and then the other side.

c.   Tilt whole head over to one side and then the other.

d.   Roll the head round in a circle and then roll the other way.

Suggested Presentation of Exercise for Young Children

'Lift your chin up towards the ceiling and tell me what you can see up there.' 'Drop your chin down onto your chest, and what do you see when you look down?' (Do not ask these questions individually, but let the children call out as they wish. Keep the drum rhythm going.)

Back Exercises

a.   Round the back and drop the chin down.

b.   Pull up the back and lift the head to the centre.

Presentation

a.   'Round your back and sit in a huddle because you are very tired.'

b.   'Now you are very excited and not at all tired, so you sit up very straight.'

a.   (On repeat of the exercise) 'Why are you very tired?'

b.   (On repeat of the exercise) 'Why are you excited?'

(You may at this early stage need to give a lead. 'Are you excited because your mum is coming this afternoon?' Such suggestions will quickly prompt their own ideas.)

Shoulder Exercises

a.   Hunch the shoulders to ears, then drop down.

b.   Pull shoulders forwards, backwards, to the centre.

c.   Roll shoulders in a circle towards the back. Put hands on shoulders and circle elbows towards the back.

Presentation

a.   'Hunch your shoulders to your ears and say, "I don't care".'

b.   'Pull your shoulders forwards because you are cold; pull them back and stick out your chest.'

c.   'Roll your shoulders in a circle because it is a nice feeling.'

Arm Exercises

a. Stretch arms out to the side and then cross arms over hands on opposite shoulders. Repeat three times, then relax, arms down by sides.
b. Lift arms above head and look up. Bring arms down in front of you and move the fingers as if you are playing the piano as the arms descend.
c. Draw a circle with one arm and then the other. Draw a large circle with both arms.
d. Draw a large circle, and draw in a mouth, a nose, two eyes, hair, ears. Make the mouth happy, sad, cross; the hair curly, short, straight, etc. (*No drum beat for this exercise.*)

2. EXERCISES TO COMBINE ALL MOVEMENTS SO FAR

a. 'Sit huddled up. On the drum beat, sit up straight, lift the head and arms towards the ceiling and shout out, "Help!".' 'Why did you have to call out "Help!"?' (Children enjoy this exercise and question immensely and replies such as, 'My cat got stuck in the clouds', 'I was trying to stop stones falling on my head', were some of the answers given to me.

Finger/Hand Exercises

a. Move all fingers as if playing a piano.
b. Clench hands and open out wide.
c. Circle wrists.

(*No accompanying sounds.*) Tutor can make up many combinations of hand exercises.

Develop into Presentation: 'Pick up something very small. Hold it in your cupped hand. Stretch your hand out and it falls off. Look for it carefully and pick it up again. Put it somewhere safe. What was it in your hand?' (Many hand exercises such as this can be devised.)

3. FLOOR EXERCISES (lying down)

a. Curl into a small ball.
b. Stretch out flat and wide, lying on your back.
c. Lying on your back, draw a circle with your arms and legs in the air.
d. Move around in a circle on your back.
e. Move all your body as you wish, including face, still lying on your back.
f. Curl into a small ball.

g.   Roll onto your tummy and stretch out flat and wide.
h.   Pretend to swim as if you were in a hurry. Swim very slowly.
(*Drum accompaniment*)

4.   TRAVELLING EXERCISES
a.   Spin around on your bottom in a circle one way, and then spin around the other way.
b.   How many objects in the room can you touch before I beat the drum for you to stop (the fact that no one can count does not matter).
c.   If you hear the drum beat, move in circles.
      If you hear me clap, move in straight lines.
      This can be expanded into three different movements for 3 different sounds.

5.   MIME
a.   Feel hot, feel cold.
b.   Make rubber faces, by twisting your face into as many shapes as possible. Now make sad, happy, cross faces; a surprised look, a puzzled look.
c.   Show with your eyes that you feel frightened, brave, hungry, etc.
d.   Make your mouth show that you are miserable, happy, hungry, thinking . . .
e.   Now one person show us how you feel, it can be anything you like to feel. We have to guess the mood. Maybe you are feeling very excited or maybe a bit fed up. (Children and tutor guess.)
f.   Develop previous mime into a story told by tutor, acted out at the same time by the children. Possibly tutor will have to enact story as well the first time. For example:
      'There was a big plate of ice cream.
      The plate was round. (*Mime*) You are hungry. (*Mime*)
      Somebody has told you not to touch the ice cream.
      You look one way, then the other way. (*Mime*)
      No one is there, so you dip your finger into the ice cream. (*Mime*)
      You hear someone coming, so you jump back into your chair, looking good as gold. (*Mime*)'

6. WORDS (Prop: a toy telephone)

a.   Children dial a number and speak to an imaginary person. (This is a good way to encourage them to say who they need to communicate with.) Later this can be developed so that one child speaks to another child who assumes the role of the person the caller wants to contact.

7. A GROUP IMPROVISATION STORY

Invent a story which will include many of the movements done before. The tutor tells the story and enacts it with the children. The purpose is to achieve sequences of movement.

A sample story: Going to the Seaside

You are going to the seaside for the day. The first thing to do is make some sandwiches. Cut the bread. Put whatever you like in your sandwich. Wrap it up. Reach up into a cupboard for your swimsuit and towel. Open the front door and run to the bus stop. Put out your arm to stop the bus. Jump on. Pay for your ticket. The bus is wobbly, you nearly fall out. Goodness, this is the stop. Press the bell. Jump off. Run down to the sea. Take off your clothes, put on your swimsuit. Plunge into the water. Swim on your back and your tummy. Suddenly you begin to shiver. You run out of the water. Dry yourself all over. Put on your clothes. Now everybody has a picnic. Everyone shares the food. What did you have in your sandwich. Goodness, look at your watch. Time to catch the bus. Quick, pack up your things. Run to the stop. Put your arm out to stop the bus. Jump on. It is a smooth ride this time. Press the bell, jump off. You walk home slowly because you are tired. Knock on the door. 'Hello, Mum, I'm back.' This story has been performed by severely physically handicapped children who have adapted it to their movement potential.

8. FREE IMPROVISATION WITH MUSIC

Listen to music (so that the children have a rest). Then say, 'Do whatever you like to the music. If you want to lie or roll over, do that; if you want to wave your arms or legs, do that; if you wish to just sit still and listen, that is fine.'

9. BREATHING EXERCISES TO FINISH SESSION

From the outset show the children how to inhale and exhale through the nose with stomach contracting and extending.

Presentation

a. Take a deep breath, just as if you were filling up with air like a balloon. The air comes in through your nose. Your tummy goes out when you breath in through your nose, because the balloon is filling up with air.

b. Now the balloon is going to let the air slowly out through your nose again. You will see how when you let the air come out through your nose your tummy crumples inwards. (Gradually and naturally begin to help the children to breathe correctly in a way which will relax them after a strenuous class.) This method class is the skeleton format around and in which new ideas can be fitted in.

Further Suggestions for Future Classes

IDEAS FOR TRAVELLING GAMES

a. Touch as many things in the room as are: hard, soft, cold . . . objects made out of wood, glass . . . coloured blue, green, white . . . people with straight, curly, short, long hair (. . . before the music stops).

(Tutor decides on any of the above ideas.)

b. Move with the music. When it stops, touch: someone else, a piece of wood, a chair, something red, someone's hands with your head, someone's legs with your hands, back with your back, hands with your hands . . . and keep quite still. (Tutor decides on ideas.)

c. Move in a straight line when you hear the sound of a shaker; in a circle when you hear the drum. Stop when you hear the triangle. (Tutor can make up combinations. This is a good game to teach them to put different sounds together with different movements or floor patterns.)

d. Another version of the same idea: roll over to this sound, spin on your bottoms to the sound of . . . etc.

e. When the music stops: hide your head, hands, feet; make yourself fat, thin, tall, small, etc. (Game to help awareness of the body as a means to form shapes and for quick reflex actions.)

MIME IDEAS

Faces: Make thin, fat, screwed up, smooth . . . faces. Every kind of expression. The same idea for eyes, mouths.

Head: Drop your head because you are: disappointed, cross, sleepy, sulking . . . Turn your head because you hear a noise, you see a friend . . . Tilt your head because you are trying to make up your mind, because you can see up into the corner that way . . . Lift your head to peer over a wall . . .

Trunk: Stretch your body forward to look into a pool, stretch back to look up at a bird flying in the sky. Stretch sideways to get out of someone's way . . .

Hands: Draw in the air with your hands and fingers: a zigzag, a circle, a star, a face . . . Stroke something gently, roughly . . . Kind hands, cross hands, show with your hands how small it is, how large.

Leg & Feet: Walk or move crossly, softly, loudly. Stand or sit or lie as if you are waiting for a friend and they are late. Make your feet show that they feel tired, bouncy . . .

At the very early ages children's vocabulary is limited, but by the age of 6 most expressions demanded of them will be understood.

SUGGESTIONS FOR USE OF PROPS

Pieces of Material: Which can be: wrapped around the body, waved in the air, trailed on the ground, made into pillows, crumpled up, stretched out, used to hide in.

Small Wooden or Cardboard Boxes: To represent different objects: tables, pianos, chairs, desks, post boxes, bridges, fences, steps. To sit in as: a car, train, aeroplane . . . Wooden boxes for climbing onto, over. (Physically handicapped children are often extremely dexterous at manipulating objects.) Ask children to extemporise physically with objects such as chairs. How many ways can you climb over . . . push . . . touch with different parts of your body.

Paper Fans: To represent: tennis racquets, hats, masks, skirts. Fans are light for children who are too weak to handle heavy objects.

Small Soft Balls: To catch, to hide around the person.

Chairs: To indicate different ways of sitting: sadly, happily, fidgety . . . To represent objects in the same way as the boxes.

SUGGESTED MOVEMENT GAMES WITH PROPS

Chairs: Travel around the room and then touch the chair with foot, hand, back, nose, legs . . . when you hear the drum. (Tutor directs.)

Cardboard Boxes: Place the boxes to form a bridge. Crawl under. Push the box around. When the music stops put your head, foot, side, etc., on the box. How many different things can you do with your box before the music stops? (Give examples such as 'You can turn it on its side, put your hands in it, use it as a wash basin, cooking pot, etc.) For severely physically handicapped children small cardboard boxes can be used.

Material: Wave the material in circles. When the music stops lay the material on the floor and sit on it. The material is a river. See if you can cross the river without getting wet. Move around the room. When the music stops hide under the material.

SUGGESTED GAMES FOR CO-ORDINATION OF MOVEMENT

Games for co-ordination, quick physical response: When I beat the drum see how quickly you can: place one hand on your head and one hand behind your back. Cross your arms and lift your head. Bend one arm and stretch out your legs. Drop your head and bend your legs . . . (Again, physically handicapped children will do what they are capable of and respond quickly to adapting the instruction to their disability.) In all these suggested games there is never really a 'winner'; each person is encouraged to work at their own pace. (Drum accompaniment.)

EXTRA SUGGESTED MOVEMENT SEQUENCES

a.   Rolling and lying flat on stomach.
      Rolling and lying flat on back.
b.   Travelling lying on back. Finish in curled up position.
c.   Travelling around room on bottom using hands to lift body from ground to represent a 'jump' for the paralysed or legless child.
d.   Moving making a lot of noise.
      Moving making little noise.
e.   Moving at fast pace then curling up slowly.
      Moving slowly and stretching out into a wide shape quickly.

f.   Moving holding hands with a partner.
Moving back to back with a partner.

EXTRA SUGGESTIONS FOR ACTING IMPROVISATIONS
Become: clowns, robots, rag dolls, cars, trains, animals, doctors, nurses, balloons, balls, trees, clocks . . .
Improvisations with Dialogue
From the age of 4–6 children like to improvise with words. At this age it must be directed in a very simple way. Children move around the room and when they hear the cue of a drumbeat they stop and begin talking (with a given sentence from the tutor). Only try this with children who are ready to go on to improvising with words.
Presentation: 'Walk around the room. When you hear the drumbeat, stop, look up and call out, 'Oh, it is beautiful, I must catch it.' You are going to decide what it is you have seen when you looked up; was it a beautiful bird, feather, a balloon, soap bubbles, you were trying to catch? When you have caught it go and show it to someone else.'
Suggested sentences:
a.   Goodness, I am late. If I don't hurry I will miss it. (What are you going to miss, and where are you going?)
b.   I lost my purse, I must go back. (Where did you lose it?)
c.   Don't go into that room. (Why not?)
Suggested Improvisations with Props
a.   Material: When you touch the material something magic happens to you. Show us what the magic does to you.
b.   Chairs: You sit on the chair; when you get up you find you stick to everything.
c.   Fans: When you pick up the fan you feel very hot, when you drop the fan you are freezing.
d.   Cardboard boxes: The boxes look empty. When you put your hand inside you find exciting things that you take out.

Suggestions for Stories to Music for 3–6 year olds
If you are lucky enough to have a pianist it is often helpful to tell a story with music which allows severely handicapped children to move to it. It is not difficult to improvise stories based around particular movements you wish the children to do.

The way I used these sample stories was to tell them, and on the cue for 'music' the children enacted them. Often the first time I enacted them with the children. If there is no pianist it is more difficult, but it can be done by the tutor beating a drum or triangle instead. These stories were very much enjoyed by children in wheelchairs or lying on mats, as well as the able bodied.

1. THE ARTIST

Movement purpose: to make the arms move freely. The whole story is mimed.

> TUTOR: Once there was an artist. He was the grandest greatest artist.
> (*music; children mime*)
> Except for one thing. Every time he tried to draw a circle it turned into a square.
> (*music*)
> The artist got crosser and crosser. He threw down his brush, stamped his foot, and sat down in a big sulk.
> (*music and mime*)
> He looked up and saw a big round ball in the corner of the room. He jumped up and went to pick up the ball.
> (*music*)
> He put down on the floor a clean white sheet of paper. He put the ball on top of the paper. Then he picked up his brush and drew a circle round the ball.
> (*music and mime*)
> The artist looked at the circle he had drawn. 'Now I am the grandest greatest artist in the whole wide world,' he said.
> (*music and mime*)

2. TREACLE

Movement purpose: to achieve slow strong movement.

> TUTOR: Mary sat in a bath of black treacle. It was so sticky she had to move her legs and arms very slowly when she wanted to move.
> (*music and mime*)

Mary's mother told her to get out of the bath. 'Hurry up,' she called. Mary slowly pulled herself up and climbed out of the bath.

(*music and mime*)

Then she tried to walk across the room, but her feet kept sticking to the floor, so she had to pull them up and it was very hard work. Mary decided to crawl across the room, but then her knees just stuck to the floor. So she had to pull them up to crawl.

(*music and mime*)

'Hurry up, Mary,' called her mother. Mary was halfway across the room and dripping treacle. She shook her head, turned around, and crawled slowly back to the bath. She pulled herself up back into the bath and sat enjoying the treacle bath.

3. THE CATERPILLAR

Movement purpose: wriggling, curling and flying movements, all of which can be interpreted from a lying or chair position.

TUTOR: It was a hot sunny day. A small furry caterpillar wriggled down the path.

(*music and mime*)

It was so hot as he wriggled down the path that he decided to curl himself into a ball and go to sleep.

(*music and mime*)

He went to sleep for quite a long time. When he woke up he tried to uncurl himself but he could not because he was covered in a ball of silk. 'Oh, dear, I don't like this,' he said as he pushed his arms and legs inside the ball of silk.

(*music and mime*)

Then he remembered his mother had told him that when he found himself in a ball of silk he would be a chrysalis getting ready to become a butterfly. So he pushed out his legs, and he pushed out his arms, and he rolled over and over till suddenly the ball of silk went POP.

(*music and mime*)

Out of the ball tumbled a beautiful yellow butterfly. 'Whee!' he said, 'I have beautiful yellow wings.'

And he began to fly. He flew higher and higher until he was only a tiny speck in the sky.
(*music and mime*)

4. SHAPES

Movement purpose: arm movements for severely physically handicapped children.

TUTOR: Draw a large square in the air.
(*music and mime*)
This is a magic square for a magic picture. Draw a pointed hat for a witch. Now draw a round shape to go under the hat – that is the witch.
(*music and mime*)
Now under the witch draw a long straight line – that is the broomstick. Can you draw a shape that looks like a cat? The cat sits on the broomstick.
(*music and mime*)
Now the square you drew to make the picture in. Pull one corner of the frame and you will find it is made of rope. Pull it and wind up all the rope and throw it in the air.
(*music and mime*)
If you look up and stretch your head very high, you may just see the witch, the cat and the broomstick disappearing into the clouds.
(*music and mime*)

5. A TINY WHITE CLOUD

TUTOR: Once there was a tiny white cloud. Fluffy and round, it floated up and down across the blue sky.
(*music*)
The wind blew harder and the cloud whirled and turned and chased over the sky as happy as could be.
(*music*)
The wind stopped.
(*music*)
The cloud stopped.
(*music*)
'What I need is a friend,' he said.

So he puffed himself out to try and make himself look bigger and more important.
(*music*)
(*music for new cloud*)
He turned and saw another white cloud floating along. The other cloud cried, 'Catch me!' and they chased each other across the sky. Faster and faster.
(*music*)
Bang! . . . (*music*)
The two little clouds bumped into each other and rolled over and over.
(*music*)
A funny thing had happened. They struggled to free themselves but could not do so.
'Look at us!' they cried, for the little clouds had turned into a big black cloud.
(*music – one sound*)
Slowly now they moved across the sky.
(*music*)
'I'm afraid I shall have to leave soon,' said one part of the cloud to the other. 'You see, I am so hot I am dripping.'
'So am I,' said the other cloud. Drip drop drip drop. Pitter patter.
(*music for rain*)
Soon all there was left of the two clouds was a great big puddle of rain on the street below.

2. MOVEMENT, ACTING AND IMPROVISATION for 7-10 year olds (able and disabled)

Introduction
These sessions develop to allow children more individual opportunity for improvising and working with others in the group. These sessions contain many ideas. Plan your own programme and do not try to fit in too much in one workshop.

These workshops work equally well with able or disabled students. A tutor who has already worked with pupils who began at the 3–6 year old stage, will find these 'next stage' sessions easier to give. With mentally disabled students I would suggest that half a method class is used, or even just one or two of the ideas. At this stage I discard the formal exercises, but they can be used as a warm-up to start a class. Children should wear suitable flexible clothes – shorts, tights, loose trousers, track suits, bare feet or PE shoes. In hospitals where staff have arranged for mentally handicapped students to have the proper clothing it has made a considerable difference to their performance. 'If you dress the part you feel the part.' There is a good deal of truth in the saying. These sessions are suitable for mentally handicapped adult students provided they are mixed with some of the 'social dance' ideas in the adult workshop sessions. Whenever possible invite staff to take part. If students are in a school where it is possible to work with non-handicapped pupils, the ideal session will combine the two groups to work together. This can be stimulating for all the children, and can go towards helping prevent the segregation that often happens in their later years.

Method Class
Theme: Forbidden/Freedom
Time: 1-½ hour
Purpose: Enjoyment, stimulus, outlet for communication.
1.   Shake out each part of the body separately. (*Music*)
2.   Lie on the floor and feel different parts of the body. Don't move, just feel inwardly. Feel your toes, your feet, your ankles, your legs, your bottom, your back, stomach, shoulders, arms, hands, fingers, elbows, kneecaps, back of legs, neck, chest, face, eyes, mouth, cheeks, chin, forehead, top of head. (*Tutor speaks all this over rhythmic accompaniment of maracas or similar. Allow time for children to feel each part of the body.*)
3.   Still lying down, now move each part of the body as you wish, but only one part at a time. In other words, in isolation. When you move put all your concentration and energy in the area you are moving. For example, if you wriggle your toes, really feel the wriggle and toes. (*Tutor directs; drum accompaniment*)
4.   Tense and relax each part of the body. Tense your arms, and release; tighten your legs, and release, etc. Now tighten up the whole body as if it was a piece of elastic stretched to breaking point, make a tight sound that goes with the physical

feeling. Now release/relax the whole body and let a sound come out. (*Tutor directs; drum accompaniment*)

5. Quietly breathe in and out (as in first method class).

6. Move across the floor as you like, but as if something restricts you so that you cannot move freely (for example, your feet are tied together). Now move as if whatever hindered you has gone and you can move without any restriction. Move in as many different ways as you can. Make sounds that fit with your way of moving.

7. Stand up. Take a partner. Link yourself to your partner so that you cannot move easily. Gradually you both manage to get free of each other. (*Music*)

8. Sitting in a cardboard box, at first you feel cramped and you are restricted in moving because of the size of the box. Now you are still in the same box but you have discovered all the different movements you can do even with the limitation of the box. So despite the lack of space you are having fun. For wheelchair students, the chair represents the restricted space.

9. Perform any kind of movement that gives you pleasure. Maybe you enjoy stretching out, or shaking, or yawning or running. Just enjoy the feel of using your body. (*Music*)

10. *Mime*: Sitting down without any outward expression, feel: laughing in your stomach; excitement in your fingers; scream with your feet; surprise at the top of your head; anger in your shoulders. Now outwardly express these sensations with the different parts of your body. (*Drum cue and tutor direction*)

11. *Improvisation with dialogue and partner*: (The whole group performs at the same time. After the 'tryout', group watches individual sketches.) One person holds the cardboard box behind him. Cue from other partner: 'What is that behind your back?' The box can represent anything and a spontaneous sketch develops. For example:

'What is that behind your back?'

'It is something secret.'

'I won't tell anyone. Please show me.'

'All right. But don't break it.'

(*And so on.*)

12. *Group improvisation*: (Work in groups of four to six people.) Movement sequence where group imagines it is in a large room with many doors. At first none of the doors will

open. Then someone finds a way of squeezing out of one of them. Soon all the doors are unlocked and everybody has fun moving in and out of the room with the many doors. (*Music*) (Children rehearse this without music, although they hear the music before beginning to work on the composition.)

13.   Whole class runs or walks around the room shouting out any phrases which are connected with 'forbidden'. For example: 'You cannot do that, it is not allowed.' 'Keep off the grass.' 'Stop running.' 'Stop talking.' etc. (*To create the impetus use maracas for background noise; when you feel they have exhausted their ideas, beat the drum loudly*.) The whole group collapses onto the floor.

14.   Lie and breathe quietly.

Further Suggestions for Future Classes
The following ideas are ones that can be substituted within the method class:

SUGGESTIONS FOR WARM-UP EXERCISES
All these warm-ups are to help children realise movement qualities or abstract qualities that can be expressed through the body frame.

a.   Shake out every part of the body.

b.   Stretch out every part of the body.

c.   Move opposite parts of the anatomy at the same time. For example, move one shoulder and one ankle; stretch the neck and bend the legs; clench the fingers and stretch out the toes.

d.   Move the frame slowly, move quickly.

e.   Contract and release various parts of the body. This is not the same movement as tension and relaxation. It is a gathering together and holding of the muscles, then a controlled release.

f.   Lie and find many ways of stretching and bending the body.

g.   Standing, move parts of the body in isolation, then move the whole body, including the face, eyebrows, scalp, etc.

h.   Standing, compose as many body shapes as possible. (Develop this to as many curved shapes, small, wide, angular, etc.)

TRAVELLING FLOOR WARM-UPS

a. Use a roll (rolling body over) or run and a stretch and spin. Compose these movements into a sequence which travels across the room. You can put the movements into whatever order you wish, using the different movements as many or as few times as you decide upon, so long as you incorporate all four at least once. (*Tutor can direct any sequence.*)

b. Take the same combination and perform it at differing speeds.

c. Making use of the furniture or walls in the room, travel as you wish. When you hear the drum cue, affix yourself by your head, back, arms, feet, legs, etc. to an object. (*Tutor calls out which part is to be attached.*)

d. Move as if floundering in water, floating, wading . . . (Many different subject descriptions can be used.)

IDEAS FOR MIME EXERCISES

a. Without outward expression, feel laughter in the toes; surprise at the top of the head; fear in the knees; waiting in the back; anger in the shoulders; gentleness in the face; prickling in the hands; cold on the bottom; excitement in the stomach. Now outwardly express the feelings.

b. Facial expressions: thoughtful suspicious, proud, tired, hungry, guilty, listening. (Use eyes and mouth the same way.)

c. Hands: Hand reactions to different surfaces. For example, smooth surface, rough, silk, sacking. Hands to show reaction to sensations: heat, cold, nervousness, calm . . .

d. The back: Emotions to be expressed through the corporal expression of the back: dignity, calm, weariness, pride, aggression . . .

e. The feet: Feet positions are fun for children to express a mood or character through. Allow enough time for each foot stance to establish not merely the shape, but the character of the shape as well: stubborn, bored, shy, impatient, bouncy, heavy, awkward, assertive . . .

f. Standing positions: Waiting for something nice to happen; waiting to go into the dentist; showing off; selling; looking over the wall; looking over your shoulder; looking down in horror; looking up in wonder; astonishment; a light stance; a heavy stance.

g. Group stances: (Tutor calls out the direction and the whole group assumes their positions.) Waiting in a queue; buying tickets; in the stands at a football match; in church; standing in the rain (different ways people hold umbrellas or protect themselves from the rain); watching a fire; watching the world go by; watching each other.

CONVERSATIONAL IMPROVISATION EXERCISES

As with the younger group, begin these by moving around the room. On the drum cue, students stop, call out the phrase the tutor has given them, and freeze in a position. This is a 'warm-up' exercise to allow them time to get the feel of the phrase. After this each one finds a partner and works out a spontaneous or rehearsed sketch using the given phrase. For the first trial the group perform all together, then they watch each pair perform.

Suggested Phrases:

'What kept you so late?'
'Do you like my shoes?'
'Oh, look up there! It is wonderful.'
'Don't look down; you won't like it.'
'I told you I could do it.'
'Do you always wear it that way?'
'I can.'
'Stop it.'
'Would you like to buy one?'
'I was first in this queue.'
'Wait for me.'

SUGGESTED PROPS FOR IMPROVISATION

a. Water in a bucket: Group sits on floor in a circle. The bucket is in the middle. In turn they get up and use the water to express: the mood they are in by the way they wash their hands, faces; how they put their feet in water; the reaction when they take them out.

b. Looking in the water, finding something.

c.   Office cleaners.
d.   Window cleaners. Etc.
e.   Chairs: One chair is placed in the middle of the group. Different ways of sitting on a chair. Different sitting positions of different characters. Chair to represent other objects/situations, for example a gate, a prison, an office chair, an armchair, a school chair . . .
f.   Large plastic balls: to represent heavy weights, a globe, a crystal glass, explosives, a cheese, a weighted ball, or a light ball.
g.   Material: to: dress body with, be a dress, shirt, shawl, cloak, robe; to represent water, tightrope, screen, wall. The material can be used to form exciting shapes by two or three moving with it. Use music for this.
h.   Elastic: Each student has a piece of elastic that is 6 mm wide, joined to make a circle. Students use the elastic to form body shapes. With a partner, using legs or hands, a form of cat's cradle can be devised. This is an exciting exercise to do. Use music.
i.   A plant: to: hide behind, sell, etc. This prop will not require many suggestions from the tutor. For, simply using it as a plant, children will create exciting ideas.

For the climax of the class a group improvisation worked out and rehearsed by students, allow 15 minutes. The subject for their composition should have a connection to the 'theme' the tutor has structured the programme around. A 'group' can be four people. Let each group watch the other students work. Group work may be too difficult for physically handicapped or mentally handicapped pupils unless they are working with able children or staff.

SUGGESTED THEMES FOR SESSIONS
a.   *Movement in time* (waiting, stillness, speed). For such a theme the end group improvisation could be a sketch where the opening of the composition was to have the group positioned in 'waiting' attitudes completely still; the movement story then develops into one of speed and urgency. Given this framework children will quickly create their ideas.
b.   *Weight* (heaviness, effort, lightness, achievement).

c. *A circus* (a whole session can be based around circus movements).
d. *Surprise* (the unknown object) movements of lift, lightness could be warm-up exercises for this theme.
e. *Running away* (hiding, finding, searching).
f. *The sea.*
g. *Selling, buying* (persuasion, movements of invitation and of response).
h. *Factories* (machines, characters, movements of work).
i. *Climbing, falling* (height, effort, the result, descending, depth, awareness of space).
j. *Growth* (large, small, wide, narrow, superiority, timidity).

These 'themes' allow for dramatic improvisation, as well as concentration on particular movement qualities.

3. IMPROVISATION FOR 10–14 YEAR OLDS

Introduction

For this age group a number of suggested sessions are written in full detail as in previous Method Classes. By this stage children will be ready to work in an abstract way. Less teacher direction will be required, yet more individual help and encouragement with each child's own ideas will be demanded of the tutor. All the previous suggestions for disabled students apply equally to this age group.

Purpose of Sessions: Stimulus, enjoyment, to provoke awareness of situations, awareness of body movements, to encourage the individual to work spontaneously with a group.

From the age of 12+ some pupils will become more self-conscious. This is particularly so with physically disabled young people. Therefore the tutor needs to be sensitive to this fact and extremely flexible in changing a planned programme if the group has an 'off' day. For all groups of students it is essential to have suitable clothing and work in bare feet or PE shoes, unless the disability makes this impractical.

Extra Suggestions for Physically Disabled Students

1. For physically handicapped adolescents sound effects can be used as structures around which improvised plays can be based and recorded on tape for others to listen to. Often when

physically handicapped children reach the age of 12 upwards, they prefer to remain in chairs. This is not to be encouraged, but if it is a definite stand taken by students, then taping plays can be enjoyable. The plays can be listened to by younger children in hospital, and so a 'library' of plays can be built up.

2.   Keep fit exercises done from wheelchairs. Students can be asked to lead the class once they have become acquainted with exercises (see page 101, Exercises for the Elderly). They then can adapt simple exercises to their own needs and abilities and also make up dance routines that can be performed from a wheelchair. Let students bring their own records/tapes for the exercises. Choreographing floor patterns for the mobile to move to can be done by drawing with chalk on a blackboard. Routines can be similar to the ones described in the mixed adult workshops, page 89.

3.   Sounds composition for wheelchair students. Improvising with different sounds using simple musical instruments, i.e. triangle, drum, sticks, bells, etc., or creating sounds with objects that are available such as tearing paper, tinkling a glass, water, door slamming, and so forth. This can be the music that a wheelchair student composes for a mobile student to choreograph a movement sequence to.

4.   Dance routines can be composed and performed from chairs. It is surprising how many routines can be devised. The students do not move the chairs, but maximum combinations of movement are performed in a seated position. Ask students each to add a sequence to the routine. Suggested music: reggae, disco, ethnic.

Method Class 1
Theme: Reactions/Responses
Time: 1–1½ hours
Purpose: To realise the different tensions and shapes the body assumes when responding to sound or movement. To respond sensitively when working as a group.

1.   Sitting in a circle. Breathing exercises.

2.   Curl the body into a ball. Slowly unfold, as each person feels they would when waking from sleep; then stretch all parts of the body including facial muscles.

3.   On the drum cue tutor calls out various shapes: square,

spiky, flat, long, straight, bent, etc. Students respond in movement to the words. It does not necessarily mean they have to form the shape called out, for it could be that the response to 'curled' would be to stretch out, for instance.

4. Students move around the room while tutor makes sounds with different percussion instruments (tambourine, maracas, drum, triangle, metronome). Students interpret the sounds into movement.

5. Take a partner. One student sits on the floor, the partner approaches from behind and touches the person in whatever manner he decides, i.e. roughly, gently, timidly pinching . . . Sitting person reacts with movement and words, or just movement. So begins a spontaneous improvised sketch. For example, partner handles sitting student roughly. Response: 'Ouch, be careful.'

6. Develop this into group working all together at the same time. Tutor calls out different crowd situations. For example: 'Fire', 'There is only one ticket left', 'He's coming', 'Don't panic', 'Be quiet' . . . Situations should be performed twice, once silently with emphasis on movement, next time with words as well.

7. Mime: a lazy character answering the door; an active character answering the door. Reactions to: the alarm clock in the morning, finding no toothpaste left in the tube, receiving a present, giving a present, listening to gossip, relating gossip (in mime). Reactions to different smells. Eye responses to: watching a TV comedy, a horror movie, a tennis match, another person opening a parcel.

8. Group improvisation (four or more): four different characters spending an afternoon at the seaside; the different ways they spend their time. For example, the character that spent all afternoon acquiring a tan, the sports fanatic, the avid newspaper reader, radio listener, etc. How do these four separate characters respond to the behaviour of each other?

9. Improvise freely to music.

10. Breathe gently.

Method Class 2
Theme: Tempo
Time: 1 hour

Prop: Metronome
1.   Breathing exercises. Concentrate on different rhythms of breathing.
2.   Standing, exercise each part of the body separately as you wish, slowly. Then exercise the whole body quickly. (*Music*)
3.   Running around the room. On the drum cue stop and call out, 'Look at the time'. Continue a spontaneous individual sketch from then on (each working individually at the same time).
4.   Qualities that effect the speed of movement. Weight, heaviness results in slow movement, lightness in speed; floating movements are movements that seem to hang in the air and are suspended. Tutor asks students to demonstrate these qualities and move at different tempos.
5.   Mime: use a metronome and vary the speed from time to time, while students mime everyday tasks such as cleaning teeth, dressing, eating, walking, cleaning the house; the tempo of the mime varies with the rhythm of the metronome.
6.   Group improvisation: a movement sequence/story which opens with the ticking of a clock.
7.   Taking a series of movements (such as a run, a leap, a spin, a collapse and a stretch) and performing them at various speeds in whatever order a student wishes to choreograph them.
8.   Moving to music how you wish, gradually decreasing the speed until stillness is achieved.
9.   Breathe gently, relaxing.

Method Class 3
Theme: Balance (A number of improvisation classes on balance should be given to physically and mentally disabled students. The tutor could enquire which students have difficulty in finding their balance.)
Time: 1 hour
Purpose: To feel how correct placement of the body can achieve balance.
Prop: Balloons
1.   Shake out each part of the body separately. (*Music*)
2.   Stretch up on toes, arms raised towards the ceiling; gradually relax all parts of the body from this position. Start by coming down on to the flat foot, let arms drop to sides; think of

a puppet held up by strings, when each string is loosed and that part of the body collapses, until the body is eventually a crumpled heap on the floor. Slowly get up and rise until in original stretched position. (*Drum accompaniment*)

3.   Breathing exercises.

4.   Travel around the room; on the cue of the drumbeat stop and freeze in different positions of balance. Focusing the eyes on a particular object will help to keep balance.

5.   With a partner, create different shapes that require balance of the body. For example, standing on toes, arms stretched upwards, change to standing on one leg, other leg stretched out in front, arms stretched out to the sides. (*Music*)

6.   With partner, improvise a short sketch where the opening words are, 'Can you hold on to me so that I don't lose my balance?'

7.   Mime: enact different situations which require the skill of balance. For example: a tightrope walker, a juggler, a waitress, carrying a pot on top of the head, carrying a pile of books . . .

8.   In small groups, compose a sequence of movements that have to do with balancing and where the members of the group have physical contact with each other.

9.   A group improvisation of dance movements where balloons are handled as part of the dance. (*Music*)

10.   Standing in original 'stretched up' position, inhale, and on exhalation collapse to the ground.

Method Class 4
Theme: Sounds
Time: 1–1½ hours

1.   Breathing exercises.

2.   Standing, move all parts of the body separately as you wish. Move all over at the same time. (*Music*)

3.   Lie on the floor. Tense and relax the body. (*Tutor directs; drum*)

4.   Standing, compose four different sounds, for example, a whistle, a shout, clicking fingers, a squeak. Now accompany that with movements that you feel fit the sound.

5.   Walk around the room in silence. When you hear the cue of a drumbeat stop and react to an imaginary noise you heard. What action do you take when you hear it? For example, it

could be a knock at the door so you open the door, or footsteps so you look round to see who is following. Remember the whole thing is silent.

6.   Take a partner. One student creates a sound. For example a bang, a stamp, a scream. The other partner has to pick up the improvisation spontaneously from that cue of sound. (Can be done with mimed movement or with words.) For example, hearing the sound of heavy footsteps, a partner might jump and say, 'Goodness, you gave me a fright.' A sketch would then develop.

7.   Sit in a circle and react individually to the sounds that I call out. (*Tutor enacts the sounds*). For example, clapping, boos, whistles, banging on door, cry of pain . . . Hearing the sound of clapping, the student might bow, or run round to a whistle, and so forth.

8.   Group improvisation. In groups of four or more, make a composition based on the sound of breaking glass. (*Tutor can pre-record sounds on a tape*)

9.   Move how you wish to different sounds of electronic music.

10.   Sitting. Breathing.

Method Class 5
Theme: Meeting Places, Opposites
Time: 1–1½–2 hours. (This session will take approx. 1½ hours or less)

1.   Lie on floor, move all parts of the body separately as you wish. But only move one part at a time, so that the movement is in isolation. Now move the whole body together. (*Tutor directs 'move your feet', etc. Drum accompaniment*)

2.   Tense and relax all the different parts of the body. (*Tutor directs 'tense your back', etc. Drum accompaniment*)

3.   Breathing exercises.

4.   Get up slowly with great control in your movements, then lie down slowly the same way.

5.   Move around the room, your movements expressing a mood. For example, joy, anger. The second time move in contrast to the first mood expressed. For example, joy then sorrow, anger then gentleness.

6.   Running around the room, when you hear the cue of the

drumbeat stop and call out a phrase that shows how you are feeling. For example, 'I am very excited', 'I am frightened'. Now take a partner. Decide who will speak first. First person says a phrase to indicate how they feel, the second person immediately adopts a contrasting mood and they improvise a small spontaneous sketch. For example: No. 1: 'I am very excited.' No. 2: 'I can't see why, there is nothing to be excited about', etc.

7.   Mime. Sitting in a circle, feel without outward expression: opposites: tall/small, shy/forward, cold/hot, friendly/un-friendly. Then stand up and mime these opposites.

8.   Group Improvisation. Work out a composition in mime or with words as you wish, where different characters are in meeting places. Each character should be in contrast to another one. (Suggestions for meeting places: fish and chip shop, surgery, pop festival, launderette.) Students choose whether or not to have music.

9.   Move to the music in contrasting ways, for example: fast, slowly, heavily, lightly, in a dream, very purposeful. Eventually still the movement until you are just creating different body shapes on the spot.

10.   Sitting in a circle, breathe gently.

Mask Work

Masks can be exciting for movement improvisation, but it is advisable to have a number of sessions with 'warm-up' exercises that will show students how to begin to use masks. It is definitely not just a matter of putting a mask on. Greater body awareness can often be achieved through mask work. Better characterisation and detailed movements tend to be results of wearing masks. At the start neutral masks that convey no particular facial expression can be used for exercises. Later there are many ways for children to make their own masks for the characters they portray. There are books on mask making in most public libraries. If the children are at school the tutor can liaise with the art department.

WARM-UP EXERCISES WITH MASKS

Before you put on the mask realise that once you wear a mask the personality you wish to portray has to be shown through the movements and shape of the body. Therefore all movements must be so clear and controlled that they 'project' themselves, because you cannot show changing facial expression. Let us take a series of warm-ups:

a.   Head Exercises with Masks: (try to feel that the head – or the mask – is leading all the movement). Turn head slowly to look one way, then the other. Look up, look down. Shake your head, nod your head. Drop the head as if you have gone to sleep. Wake up startled. Incline your head to either side. The first time perform these exercises neutrally so that there is no personality, the second time allow the movements to have character.

(Allow some students to watch the others. Much can be learnt from the beginning by seeing others work. One of the most common faults is making all movements on too small a scale. Never hurry mask work.)

b.   Body Exercises with Masks: Stand in a position of greeting; show that you are not too happy that you are about to be embraced; stand in position of depression, alertness, stillness; laugh silently; listen intently; reprove someone.

c.   Walk: looking around, searching, being followed, a jaunty walk, a sinister walk; walk like an older person, a child, a clown, juggler, tightrope walker, singer, TV announcer, politician.

d.   Hand Exercises Wearing Masks: feeling something square, small, round; painting a picture; breaking through a hole in the wall and coming out the other side; constructing something; taking something apart; tearing something; wrapping up a parcel.

e.   Feet Exercises and Masks: (sitting on chair, arms folded) circle ankles; tap feet impatiently; swing legs in different ways of different characters; legs outstretched, lean body and head forward.

(Standing) walk on toes, walk with toes turned in/out, take large strides, then stop; wiggle fingers and toes at same time with head looking up.

METHOD CLASS WITH MASKS
Theme: Characterisation
Time: 1 hour

1. Breathing exercises.
2. Standing, shake out each part of body. Shake out everything. (*Drum or music*)
3. Compose many different body shapes. (*Drum*)
4. Develop stances, walks and sitting positions of different characters: fussy, bossy, shy, funny, fidgeting people.
5. Put on the mask and take one of the previous characters and perform everyday actions in the manner of the person. For example, eating, dressing, getting into bed . . .
6. With a partner, one wearing mask the other not, (take masks off frequently if students get too hot wearing them). The mask-wearer is the real person, the non-masked partner is the reflection in the mirror. Mirror movements. Change roles. (*Music*)
7. Group improvisation. Theme of sequence: 'waiting'. Some of the group wear masks, others do not. Perform a dance story sequence. (*Music*)
8. Take off masks and shake out all over. Move swiftly around room. On drum cue, jump into air and collapse on the floor.
9. Breathe gently.

Further Suggestions for Future Classes

IDEAS FOR OTHER SKETCHES
1. Making excuses (in order not to be involved in situations).
2. Accusation (accuser, supplicant, mediator).
3. Telephone conversations (where the dialogue is so desscriptive that we can imagine the character on the other end of the line.

EXERCISES FOR MIME WITHOUT USING ARMS OR HANDS
1. Walking in the park with hands in pockets, brushing leaves away from feet.
2. Wet nail polish, which means you have to shut drawer with other part of body, or answer the phone in another way.
3. Random walk exercise: as the class walk around the room, tutor calls out different scenes for them to look at. Students must keep walking all the time, although changing the movement of the head and eyes. For example, 'a fairground', 'a tennis match', 'a zoo', 'a mountain'.

PROPS TO CONVEY MOODS AND EMOTIONS
1. Tossing a beanbag between two people indicates the feeling of passing the buck.
2. Unwrapping a parcel to indicate anger/sorrow.
3. Tearing up paper to indicate boredom.
4. Scribbling with chalk = anxiety.
5. Closing a book = finality.
6. Knitting = tranquillity.

SUGGESTED RECORDED SOUND EFFECTS
For the opening sounds of a group improvisation, storms, rain, bells ringing, scraping, hammering, breaking glass, etc., can open sketches.

POEMS
Reading a poem as the basis for a whole session, of if not for the entire session, for a group improvisation. Often if the poem is read with its right rhythm, the children can create their own music for an improvisation by claps, stamps, humming, etc. The tutor could invite the students to write poctry which expresses movement for a later session.

ART GALLERIES/MUSEUMS
Organising visits to art galleries and museums and afterwards during a workshop recreating the shapes of sculptures or paintings. Most art galleries and museums, if given prior notice, will welcome disabled students and go out of their way to make the visit a success.

LIVE DANCE
It is important to take students to the theatre to see different dance forms performed; mime also can be an enriching experience for the group.

ADULT WORKSHOPS FOR ABLE AND DISABLED STUDENTS

Introduction
The following improvisation sessions are ones that I have given to disabled students, hospital staff, and medical students and

social workers, or they are sessions that I gave at the Little Theatre in London to actors, dancers and anyone interested in improvisation. They are suitable for students from 14 upwards.

The purpose of all these sessions was to draw out from the students: (a) imaginative ideas; (b) awareness of their own movement potential; and (c) to loosen up and not be inhibited by improvisation.

Often at first staff in the caring professions found such an approach difficult. Once their initial reserves were overcome they became very creative and exciting to work with. Many students acknowledged that at the end of an eight-week course (one two-hour session a week) these workshops had enabled them to realise their own talents in movement and to see the value of this approach. They admitted that at first it was an effort to treat such sessions seriously, partly because of their rigid timetable and partly because the words 'dance' or 'improvisation' seemed irrelevant to their disciplines.

The selection of sessions contains ideas that can be used easily by someone with a limited dance experience. The written sessions last for two hours. This is the minimum time that I like to work with adults. However, anyone wishing to give only a one-hour class can take some of the ideas and plan a shorter programme.

The sessions can be used with psychiatric patients, physically handicapped adults and adolescents.

It is essential to plan in advance. Know exactly what props, music, etc., you will require. Try to memorise the order of the programme, but always have it written down as well. Be flexible. If the students do not respond well to an idea, cut it out. Shorten the programme if the group's concentration goes. Most important of all, enjoy yourself and feel at ease when giving the session. In that way all of you will have fun.

For some of the mentally disabled some of these workshops will be too difficult, especially if they have not been introduced to dance from an early age. Make sure that students wear flexible clothing wherever possible. Do not expect a handicapped young woman wearing a dress to lie on the floor and perform leg exercises without feeling inhibited. If there is a problem in finding funds for buying suitable gear I suggest that someone could approach local tradesmen for donations towards the

The author giving a dance session to physically handicapped children during the early years of her work.

MENTALLY HANDICAPPED STUDENTS' WORKSHOP

Right: A student dancing to represent joy.

Below right: Creating a body shape of 'firmness'.

Below left: Dancing to the theme of 'firmness'.

Right: A student and the author working to create body shapes and space.

Below: Another interpretation of body shapes and space.

PSYCHIATRIC STUDENTS' WORKSHOP

Students working on linked movements.

Linked movements.

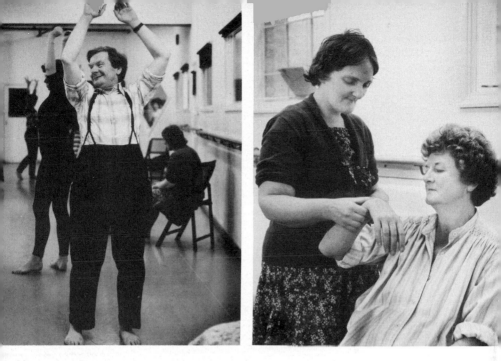

Mirrored movements.

Being handled by the partner.

A student relaxes, allowing his partner to position him.

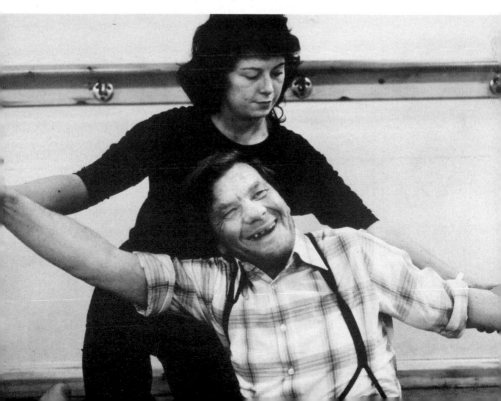

A student positions her partner.

Students working on making the body an extended line with part of the studio.

Extending the line with a partner.

WORKSHOPS
FOR
PHYSICALLY
DISABLED
STUDENTS

Making abstract shapes with
material.

Making abstract shapes with
elastic.

op left: Forming sculptures
ith material.

op right: A group makes
bstract shapes with elastic.

entre: The feel of 'stretch'
s a group.

ight: The author works
ith a visually handicapped
tudent, feeling 'stretch'.

WORKSHOPS FOR CHILDREN IN HOSPITAL

Mime: cleaning the teeth.

Mime: accusation.

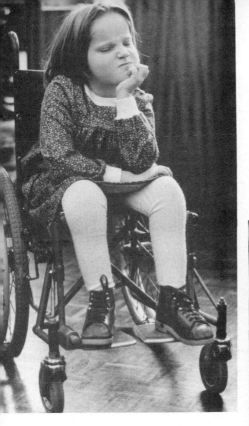

Above: Mime: thinking hard.

Right: Dance movement theme 'reaching'.

Left: Mirroring your partner

Below left: Tying the body in a knot.

Below right: Reaching.

Above right: Moving as if 'ready to go'.

Below right: Dancing for fun

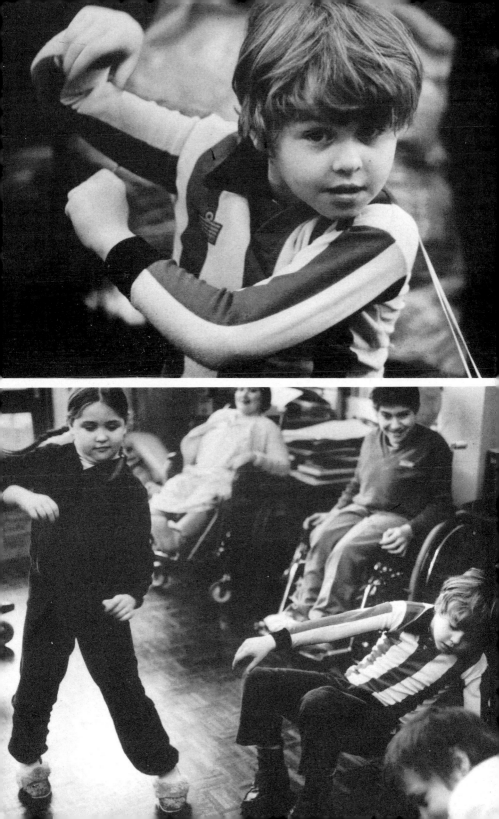

MOVEMENT WORKSHOP
FOR
ELDERLY PEOPLE

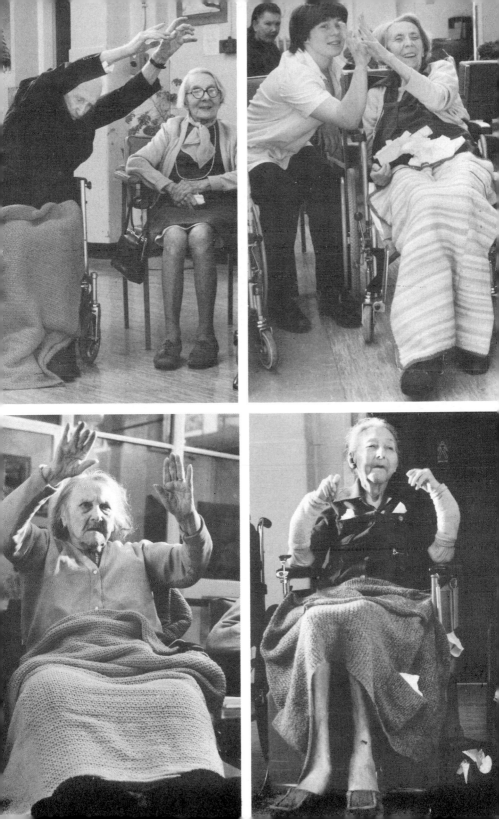

A session in a women's prison.

cost. This has proved successful in a number of instances. The same need for suitable clothes applies to psychiatric patients. Never force anyone to put on something he or she does not want to wear. Bare feet or light weight flat shoes should also allow for a better opportunity to move correctly.

Older psychiatric or mentally handicapped patients in particular may wish to work from chairs arranged in a large circle around the room, rather than sitting or lying on the floor. The same movements I have suggested can be adapted to this situation. Demonstrate all the movements and directions you wish the students to achieve. Clear and simple examples are easy to follow. You may find able and disabled students reticent at first about using spoken dialogue or sounds. It is important to overcome this shyness because the release of sound can help the release of inhibitions and tensions. Again demonstrate yourself first, calling out a phrase you wish them to use.

Wherever possible arrange for disabled students to work outside their surroundings and sometimes with able bodied dancers. Contact the nearest school of dance, college or adult education institute. Invite these places either to send interested students to join in a session taking place in the hospital/institution, or better still to arrange for classes to take place in their surroundings.

There is a description on page 89 of the mixed workshops I have given. You will find a mixture of people can be stimulating for everyone.

Always invite staff to participate, and always have two members of staff in the room when taking a session in case there are any problems. This applies when working with disabled students.

Adult Workshop 1
Theme: Breath/Stretching Movements
Time: 2 hours
Music: Record player or tape recorder; percussion instrument.
Props: Pieces of elastic, each piece tied together to form a circle.
1.   Group stands in circle, moving rhythmically on the spot to the music. Each student calls out his or her name. Move

inwards in a circle, clapping. Move outwards, holding hands, and making eye contact with as many of the group as possible. (*Suggested music: disco, reggae*)

2.   Standing anywhere in the room, stretch all the parts of the body separately (remember fingers, toes, face, scalp, etc.). (*Music*)

3.   Breathing exercises (see p. 28). Sitting on floor cross-legged, repeat each stage four times.

4.   Using Stage 1 of the breathing, make a movement of contraction (folding in movement) on the inhalation, and a stretched movement on the out breath. While the body is empty of breath, remain still (or suspended) in whatever position you happen to be in. Allow the student to feel the breath is not only providing the impetus, but is the music as well. (Do not hurry this part of the session, as it would cause tension.)

5.   Lie on the floor on back. 'Feel' (with no outward movement) separate parts of the body stretched. In other words, "isolate" all the feeling to one particular area of the body. (*Tutor directs, i.e. 'feel that your facial muscles are stretched,' etc.*)

6.   Now physically stretch every part of the body, and contract. Work as you wish. For example, begin with the toes, or you may prefer to begin with the scalp and forehead and facial muscles first. (*Tutor directs; drum accompaniment*)

7.   Stretch because you feel contentment; stretch because you are being pulled out.

8.   Now take a piece of elastic and stretch the body as you stretch the elastic. For example, put your feet in the elastic and stretch it out in different directions.

9.   Walk around the room saying phrases which would make you stretch out. For example, 'Can you reach it?', 'Reach up and you can get it', 'Jump up and you will reach it'. Keep walking as you are talking, but visualise each sentence.

10.   Develop a movement sequence with a partner where the body has to reach out. (*Music*)

11.   Group sits in a circle. One person goes into the centre and, creating her own rhythm, performs a series of reaching/ stretching movements. Another joins in, picks up the rhythm that the first person is working with, and begins to interact with

her. Change people over in circle. Rest of the group is clapping and stamping the rhythm.

12.   Stretching with objects. Using the following props (each student selects): material, shoes, gloves, a chair, chalk. Using their chosen prop, students make a composition where the focus is on using the prop to aid reaching or stretching movement. For example: chalk, where the body reaches out to draw and becomes part of the drawn line; shoes, where the focus will be on legs and foot movements; material, under which student is hidden forming sculptural shapes.

13.   A group improvisation. Compose a dance sequence from: spins, runs, stretches, contracted movements and jumps. Have no more than six in each group. (Listen to the music first, before rehearsing.) Physically handicapped students may have to create the illusion of these movements, perhaps even from a wheelchair. It is possible to do this.

14.   Lie on floor, breathing gently; relax (see suggestions for relaxation).

Adult Workshop 2
Theme: Touch
Time: 2 hours
Purpose: Awareness of the importance of physical contact; to help overcome inhibitions and enjoy a tactile session.

1.   Standing in a circle, move all parts of the body separately. Move as you wish, i.e. stretch, bend, shake, twist. . . Then move the whole body together. (*Tutor demonstrates with class. Music*)

2.   Sitting. Breathing exercises. (*Drum accompaniment*)

3.   Lie on the floor on back and feel the surface of the floor with different parts of the body. Tutor directs: 'Feel the floor with your back, with the back of your head, your arms, your buttocks, back of your legs. Roll over, feel the floor with your chin, your chest, your head, etc.'

4.   Sitting up, feel yourself with as many different parts of yourself as you are able. For example, your forehead can touch your knees, your toes can feel your calves, your elbows can feel your hips, etc. The idea is that all parts of the body can be used in a tactile way. (This is important to stress for the physically handicapped.)

5.   Standing and travelling around the room, touch different objects or surfaces in the room without any contact involvement. In other words, you touch but do not feel the sensation of the surface against the skin. The second time, walk round and spend time touching each surface in order to get the sensation. (*Drum or tambour accompaniment*)

6.   Running around the room, on a drumbeat cue stop suddenly and hold on roughly to the nearest person. Repeat this, but hold someone gently.

7.   Take the partner you are holding. Spontaneously (either sitting, lying or standing) touch each other. React spontaneously to the touch. Remember, you can make contact with every part of the body.

8.   Now get tangled up with your partner and move into a series of intertwined positions. (*Music*)

9.   Mime. Feel inwardly (without any outward movement) the following: smooth, soft, rough, prickly, water, snow, hot surfaces, cold surfaces. Now outwardly mime these tactile responses.

10.   Improvise a sketch between two people where touch and dialogue are involved. Show how you can help change a situation by physical contact. For example, the imaginary character Mrs Smith is very depressed, having received bad news. You go to Mrs Smith and say, 'Mrs Smith, come and have a cup of tea, don't cry.' If you gently and reassuringly add some physical contact with her that will encourage her to move, it will be far more efficacious. Or, for example, a character wishing to move away can be restrained by reassuring handling. So create quick sketches that focus on this aspect of handling.

11.   Compose a group dance where the dancers eventually link into each other like a jigsaw puzzle. Leave a space for a missing piece of the jigsaw. This small piece keeps trying to fit into the wrong shape. In the end it finds the slot. This can be done humorously and with words. When the missing piece fits incorrectly the others say, 'Don't be stupid, not here.' and when the missing piece comes to rest, 'Ah, like so.' (Obviously the dialogue is improvised by the students.)

12.   With a partner, choreograph a sequence of movements where the students keep in physical contact with a specific part

of the body. For example, back to back, side by side, hands, feet, bottoms. (*Music*)

13. Move/dance freely with speed to music. When music fades sink to the ground and breathe gently. Relax and reflect on the sensations you experienced during the session.

Adult Workshop 3
Theme: Body Shape
Time: 2 hours
Purpose: Awareness of the body's potential to create various shapes; awareness of how movements of body shapes choreograph a form that relates to the environment and floor pattern.
Props: Material, blackboard chalk

1. Standing in a circle, move/exercise all parts of the body separately. Move the whole of the body together. (*Music*)
2. Breathing exercises.
3. Develop the breathing exercises by inhaling and then forming a body shape on the exhalation. (*Drum accompaniment*)
4. Standing, take a look at the room. Form shapes that blend with the surroundings. For example, form a line that relates to the corners and ceiling. Notice the surface of the walls, where the windows are placed. Perhaps by working against the wall (being in physical contact with it) create an extended shape. Rehearse silently, then perform your composition with music.
5. Trace out different floor patterns, travelling. For example, zigzag into a circle into a zigzag into a series of dots (by jumping) into a straight line across the circle. When rehearsed, perform with music.
6. Take a partner. One student is a shop window dummy. Place your partner in any pose you wish to put her. (The partner must be completely relaxed for this exercise.) Change over.
7. Sit in a circle with closed eyes. Feel without outward movement that you become any of the shapes the tutor calls out, e.g. square, spiky, round, angular, curved. Then form the shapes. (*Tutor directs*)
8. In groups of three, form shapes with pieces of material. As you fold it, let the body flow into the folding movement. Cover the form to create sculptured effects. (*Music*)
9. Group composition. Represent crystal glass that starts as

being blown out into a beautiful design. Then the whole shatters and the splinters break away. Still each piece has a clear beautiful movement that finally rests somewhere in the room. (*Music*)

10.   Standing in a circle, one person draws a shape on the floor with blackboard chalk. The next person interprets the shape into a body movement, then draws a line for the next student.

11.   Move freely to music, incorporating some previous ideas of the session.

12.   Sit and breathe quietly.

Adult Workshop 4
Theme: Body Rhythm
Time: 2 hours
Purpose: To become aware of your own rhythm; to discover if your everyday speed suits you; to correct rhythm distortions.

1.   In a circle, warm up all separate parts of the body with changing rhythms, eg. slow, fast, very fast, very slow, suspended.

2.   Breathing exercises (sitting). Then change the rhythm of breathing as you wish.

3.   Lie on the floor. Tense and relax separate parts of the body at various speeds. Tutor directs.

4.   Travel around the room at varying tempos. In between, achieve stillness.

5.   Standing still looking at an imaginary clock or watch, speak (aloud) phrases that come to mind relating to the clock. Develop this by travelling around the room, talking about time as you do in daily life. For example, 'Hurry up', 'We haven't much time', 'What is the hurry?', 'Slow down'.

6.   Mime. Sitting in a circle, eyes closed, feel time. Tutor calls out words such as 'a year', 'waiting', 'a second', 'endless'.

7.   At tutor's direction call out body shapes that are affected by time. For example, 'waiting', 'urgency', 'boredom', 'leisure', 'suspended'. Freeze in each position.

8.   Now, having established your natural rhythm, compose a movement sequence that changes tempo but returns to the original rhythm at the end of the composition.

9.   Sitting in a circle, one student goes to the centre and moves at her own speed. The rest of the group picks up the rhythm

either by clapping, stamping, clicking fingers, etc. Keep changing the person in the centre.

10.   Develop this idea so that the student in the centre has to pick up a rhythm that the group has chosen (one person sitting beats out a rhythm, the rest of the group pick it up and clap, the centre person then translates this into movements.

11.   Mime. Perform everyday actions such as walking, brushing hair, dressing, etc. Perform an action in different stages of life, i.e. as a small child, adolescent, middle years, elderly, very old. Take care to observe the different tempos at which an action would be done, and also the pace of breath.

12.   Group composition. Use rolls, spins, runs, pauses, jumps, slow walks, stretches and bends. Vary the tempo. First time no music, second time with music.

13.   Lie quietly. Relax.

Adult Workshop 5
Theme: Space/Sound
Time: 2½ hours
Purpose: To be aware of movement in relation to space. To recognise how sound can fill and change the space. To improvise and adapt movement to a limited space.

1.   Standing. Warm up the body as if it is confined to a small area. Now move as you like, allowing the movements the freedom of a large area. (*Music*)

2.   Breathing exercises. Be aware of the sound you make when breathing.

3.   Lie on the floor and simply feel the space around you. Notice the height of the ceiling, the distance from the window, your length of body, how near you are to the next person.

4.   Now move as you wish in relation to the space in the room. For example, perhaps you look at the angle of the ceiling and create a body shape that extends the line of the room, or you notice the width of the room and create a body shape that becomes part of the width.

5.   Stand up and travel around the room; notice your closeness to or distance from others in the room. When you hear the drumbeat, block everything and only be aware of yourself in the room.

6.   Make shapes and sounds that give you the feeling of

frustration because there is a lack of space. Now change and make sounds and movements that give you a feeling of space and pleasure.

7.   With a partner, place yourselves in a situation which restricts your movements. For example, sitting in a box, or draw a chalk circle around yourself. You can only move within the circle. You are tied up and only your head is free. The first time, improvise as if you are frustrated verbally and physically by the confined area. The second time you come to terms with the situation and find many ways of moving that you enjoy even in that limited space.

8.   Mime. Sitting in a circle, feel: lost, alone, in a crowd, cramped up, too much noise, stillness, rolling space, your body shaking with mirth. (*Tutor directs*) Now outwardly show these experiences.

9.   Group improvisation. Mime an improvisation where the sound effects are important to the sketch. For example, tearing of paper, clicking fingers, whistling. Now perform the same sketch and take away the sound effects. See how much more important the area you work in becomes. If you take away the sound it is necessary to use the space fully in order to give strength to the story.

10.   Hold different parts of the body as if they were a pencil and direct their movement. For example, let the left hand pick up the right arm and move it. Push the head where you wish it to go. Turn the trunk into different positions as if it were incapable of moving by itself. If you have long hair use this to move with the space.

11.   Now move freely as you wish but use different levels of height. For example, close to the floor, stretched up, middle level. Rehearse without musical accompaniment. The second time perform with music. Notice the different qualities of movement feeling you have with or without music.

12.   From a wide stance slowly contract into a small crouched position, head tucked in, then slowly move again to lie on the floor stretched out on your back.

13.   Relax and breathe gently.

Adult Workshop 6
Theme: Shape/Energy

Time: 1½–2 hours
Props: Pieces of rope; 1 long piece large enough for the
           whole group to hold.
1.   Standing in a circle, move each part of the body separately.
(*Music*)
2.   Move all the body together (do not forget the facial
muscles). (*Music*)
3.   Breathing stages 1 and 2.
4.   Think about the energy inside yourself and breathe in and
out, being very aware that these breaths are creating an energy
for yourself. As you exhale perform strong slow movements
with any part of the body you wish to use. Feel the energy in the
movement.
5.   Travelling round the room, 'lead' with different parts of
the body. For example, lead with the elbows – that means the
elbow has the energy and impetus to lead your body as it travels
around the room. You could lead with your hips, your head,
your back. Try to imagine that all the energy is coming from
the 'leading' part of the body.
6.   Sit quietly. When you hear the drum cue, use one part of
your body to explode with movement and energy, hold that
explosion of movement for a second, and then completely
relax. On the next cue, explode with a different part. For
example, from a relaxed hand position your fingers might splay
out, or your knees might bend, your trunk flop over, but such is
the energy that it will look to the audience like an explosion.
This does not mean you have to perform a movement so
sharply it could cause you to injure yourself – energy can be
very controlled.
7.   Travelling around the room on the drum cue, create
different shapes with the nearest person to you. Feel the same
energy in the shape, remain still until you hear the cue to travel
again.
8.   Lie or sit and rest. Listen to the music and visualise
different shapes: triangles, squares, circles, stars, long lines;
in your mind colour the shapes. (*Tutor plays appropriate
music*)
9.   Take a piece of rope, place it on the floor in a shape (if you
are in a chair, tell your partner to hold it in the shape you
wish). Now move within the rope shape, trying to improvise.

You can touch the rope with different parts of the body if you wish. (*Music*)
10.   As a group, hold the large piece of rope together and create different shapes. Then one person goes into the rope shape and dances; when he returns the shape changes and another person moves in. (This is too difficult if the students are severely disabled.)
11.   Travel around the room and on the drum cue explode with energy as you wish, and create a loud sound or word to accompany the movement shape. Repeat, creating new sounds and movements.
12.   Take a piece of rope each and improvise a dance sequence to the music you heard when you were resting in the session.
13.   Relax. Talk-through relaxation by the tutor.

Adult Workshop 7
Theme: Awareness of the body as means of communication
            (including awareness of tension, relaxation, energy).
Time: 2 hours
Purpose: To heighten an individual's realisation of the way movement used with the correct energy can communicate, sometimes better than words. To show how few people use the body to its full potential. (The introduction to this session should be an explanation of the purpose, also emphasising the need to pay attention to correct breathing for the release of energy.)
1.   Standing in a circle, move all parts of the body separately as you wish, but in a neutral way. In other words, the movements are *from* you but have no personality. Now exercise/move all the body together, but this time with the awareness that the movements are *part* of *you*.
2.   Breathing exercises. Perform these incorrectly as if you are in tension. Now correct the distortions. As you breathe feel how the breath gives you the impetus to release energy.
3.   Lie on the floor on your back. Feel the body pressed into the floor (no outward movement). Feel the knees, tips of fingers, top of the head, mouth, stomach, backs of the knees, calves, buttocks, shoulders, feet, eyes, ears. (*Tutor directs*)
4.   Tense and relax each part of the body separately. Then

tense and relax the whole body. (*Tutor directs, drum accompaniment*)

5.   Travel around the room with tension, correct and travel with ease. Sit with tension, sit at ease. (*Tutor can suggest many other everyday actions to be performed in this way*)

6.   Perform movements that do not quite 'reach the end'. In other words, you do not use the maximum potential and energy to stretch, or bend, or roll. Say hello with warmth, no with conviction, shake hands, wave goodbye, smile, etc. It is all half-hearted. Now repeat the same actions reaching right to the end of the movement. (My dance instructor used to say, 'when you stretch out your hands, go beyond your finger tips.')

7.   The previous exercise helps us to realise how in most instances we can stretch ourselves 'that much more'. That the energy can flow from any part of the body. Let us take an exercise which is best described as an 'explosion of movement'. On the drum cue, direct all the energy into one part of the body and perform a movement. For example, all the energy into a movement with the shoulders, the hips, the back, the face . . . After the 'explosion' return to a neutral relaxation. (*Tutor directs thus: 'take the energy into a hip movement'. Drum cue*)

8.   Travelling around the room, develop this exercise so that you 'lead' with different parts of the body because the energy focus is there. Travel leading with the hips, the fingers, the back of the head, the stomach, the feet. Change to another part of the anatomy when you have experienced this 'lead' situation satisfactorily. (*Music*)

9.   Mime. Sitting in a circle. Pull the face about as if it were rubber. Sit and with no outward expression feel neutral, tense, relaxed, pain in the hands, afraid to move the neck, scorn in the forehead, truth in the eyes, disapproval with the mouth, approval in the smile, irritation, acceptance. Now show these outwardly. Notice how much more movement is required in the negative emotions.

10.   Group Improvisation. Compose a dance sequence where the opening movements are neutral and lack energy. Gradually the composition becomes full and dynamic. (Remember energy does not necessarily mean speed or violence. Energy can be exuded from stillness.) The piece should end with the group forming a strong shape.

11.   Take a roll, a spin, stretch, contractions, runs and stops. Choreograph these movements (working individually). Perform one neutrally; then a second time with your own movement quality.

12.   Sit on the floor and breathe gently. Lie on the floor and feel completely neutral.

Adult Workshop 8

Theme: Quality of movement, including distortion and correction, effort and ease, projection.

Time: 2 hours

Purpose: To make the student aware of the various qualities of movement; to help correct incorrect movement; to emphasise the value of projecting.

1.   Standing in a circle, exercise all parts of the body separately. Now move all parts of the body together. (*Music*)

2.   Lie on the floor; tense and relax various parts of the body. (*Tutor directs*)

3.   Breathing exercises.

4.   Stand. Move how you wish, but as if out of control. On the drum cue try to stop as if you find it difficult to do so.

5.   Make a series of balanced positions. Feel your centre of gravity, which gives you your equilibrium. In other words, in whatever balanced position you take, feel the body's complete alignment. (*Slow music*)

6.   Travelling around the room move with varying quality. Change the quality when you hear the drum cue. Types of movement qualities suggested: staccato, deliberate, heavy, weak, light and flowing, unco-ordinated, poised, with effort, effortless. (*Tutor directs*)

7.   In groups of four, take four different movement qualities and choreograph a composition. (*Music*)

8.   Sitting on the floor, again feel your centre of gravity. Take a series of balanced positions on the floor. For example, lying on your side, one leg in the air, balancing on a knee, etc. Deliberately lose your balance in the positions. The second time, repeat and hold your balance.

9.   Mime. Feel, with no outward expression: leaping, spinning, giddiness, walking, zigzagging, movements that are vague (indirect), movements that are certain (direct). Now

mime outwardly body shapes and facial expressions which represent these qualities. (*Tutor calls out words, for example: uncertain = indirect, giddy = feeling faint, drunk =zigzag*)

10.   Direct and indirect movements, with hands and eyes. Firstly let the eyes rest on people and objects in the room, but the gaze is constantly changing and never focuses long enough to make any proper contact. The second time the gaze is direct, the eyes working like a camera; from one object it directly transfers to another picture. Repeat this with hands pointing to different places, and then with the head. (*Drum beat for change of focus*)

11.   Standing, perform everyday actions such as brushing hair, cleaning teeth, eating. First in a negative manner where the concentration is not really on the action. The second time reverse the situation.

12.   Group improvisation. In a group, use different movement qualities and choreograph a dance sequence. The quality of the movement is direct and therefore projects out to the audience. Each movement must reach or go beyond the end. The whole torso and face must be alive. The result should be vital and expressive. (*Music*)

13.   On your own, perform any movements you enjoy doing.

14.   Breathe gently. Relax completely.

Adult Workshop 9

Theme: Improvisation with objects, and using the body as the object.

Purpose: To stretch creative ideas through working with objects; awareness of timing and sensitivity in responding to working with partners or in a group.

Props: Newspaper, bean bags, boxes, bucket of water, chairs.

1.   Stand in a circle and warm up all parts of the body separately. (*Music*) Now touch yourself with yourself. For example, the head can touch the knees, toes can touch the hands, elbows the stomach, chin the chest, shoulders the ears, etc. (*Music*)

2.   Lying on back, direct the energy and move as tutor instructs. For example, 'Contract the stomach, stretch the toes

and fingers, curl the trunk, twist the face, tighten the buttocks, tighten the calves, turn the head.'

3.   Stand. With the use of a chair, discover ways of stretching or curling up, always keeping in contact with the chair.

4.   Handling at a distance. (This is an exercise for sensitivity and timing with your partner.) Stand on the opposite side of the room from your. partner. One student represents an inanimate shape of rubber. The other partner is the sculptor. The sculptor moulds the form into any size or shape he wishes to. The direction and response should be almost simultaneous if the partners are sensitive to each other's timing. An example of how the sculptor could begin would be thus: directing with his hands he can stretch out the form, flatten it, roll it towards him, contract it up, elongate it, smooth it, . . . After a time partners change roles. (*No accompanying sound*)

5.   Mime. Feel (but do not show outwardly) as if you are a broom being handled roughly; a pair of shoes well worn by a tramp; faded flowers in a vase; flowers in full bloom; a goldfish in a bowl; yourself looking into the bowl. Now take one or two of these suggestions and move to represent the idea.

6.   Take any small object you may have with you and discover different ways of travelling around the room carrying it (bean bags are useful). (*Music*)

7.   Game: Reaction to objects. Sitting in groups of four to six. One person handles the bean bag in any way he wishes, and then puts it down. The next person reacts to the first handling by using the bean bag as she wishes, and so on. This exercise does not have to go in turn but should be spontaneous. Again, a group learns to time sensitively to each other.

8.   Group improvisation in dance (groups of four). Use a bucket of water as the focal prop. The dance is about reactions to touching the water. (*Rehearse, then perform with music*)

9.   Exercise with paper (groups of two). One person takes a sheet of paper and folds or crumples or tears it, whatever she wishes to do. The other student must translate the action into movement, and ends up in the shape in which the newspaper was left. Sounds can be used instead of movement to translate the action.

10.   Paper tearing for story telling (groups of two). This is a good exercise for deaf students. One student tears paper and

folds it to represent an object, for example an ice cream cone. The other student continues the story by folding another piece of paper to represent something connected with the first idea (e.g. summer, so forms paper into a ball). First partner takes both pieces of paper and responds (e.g. makes a bat to hit the ball), and so the story unfolds.

11. Develop the previous exercise by students representing objects and telling a story. Work in groups of four or five. For example, one student tells a simple story with four objects in it (e.g. a scarecrow, a plough, the earth, the sun). The four students each represent one of these things and enact the story as it is told by the fifth person. An example of how the story could begin would be: 'The earth was hard and cold. A scarecrow stood protectively in the middle of a brown field, the wind making his clothes flap about him. A plough began to loosen the hard earth. Then a wintry sun emerged from behind the clouds, the scarecrow stopped waving about . . .' (This exercise can provide exciting creative results.)

12. Group improvisation. A group dance where two cardboard boxes are used. The boxes keep changing their identity. (*Music*)

13. Finish the session by moving neutrally, no personality or representation. Gradually sink to the floor.

14. Breathe gently, relax.

(This class has enough ideas to cover two sessions.)

Adult Workshop 10
Theme: Colour
Time: 2 hours
Purpose: To be aware how colour can stimulate or depress. Awareness of the relationship between colour and space. To develop abstract ideas from a colour.
Props: Paint or chalk

1. Standing in a circle, shake out all parts of the body separately. Then shake the body as a whole. (*Music*)

2. Sitting, do breathing exercises. Allow different colours to come into your thoughts as you breathe.

3. Travel around the room. On a drum cue the tutor calls out a colour. Students react as they wish to the word. For example 'blue' could cause the reaction of looking up into the sky;

'green' could be associated with grass; or the response can be completely abstract.

4.   Make a shape and call out a colour that gives you the feeling of being hemmed in. Form a shape and call out a colour that gives you the feeling of space.

5.   With a partner, begin a spontaneous sketch/dialogue. The opening word must be a colour. For example, 'pink'. Second partner: 'Pink, do you have to choose it in pink?' First partner: 'Well I suppose you would have given them a black one . . .'

6.   Mime. Sitting, feel with no outward expression (as tutor calls out): grey (roads or too much space), green (plants, growing, height), red (excitement, hemmed in, exotic, a room), black (blank, blot, shope, space), white (cold, clear, mountain, flat), orange (circles, oranges, laughter), mauve (blocks, corridors).

7.   Take one of the colours and choreograph a movement sequence, bearing in mind that it is the colour that stimulates your ideas. Use the words as well, if you wish.

8.   In groups of four, use the paint or chalk and draw or paint shapes and lines that the colours suggest to you. Then translate the drawing into movement and make a dance. Rehearse. (*Music*)

9.   Group improvisation. Take some of the separate compositions done before and link them. (*Same music as 8*)

10.   Breathe gently, lie and see your favourite colours. Relax.

Adult Workshop 11
Theme: Plants and Growth
Time: 1½–2 hours
Props: Plants of different shapes.

1.   Standing in a circle, move each part of the body separately. Then move the whole body. Do not forget to exercise the facial muscles and the head. (*Music*)

2.   Breathing stages 1, 2, 3 (see page 28).

3.   Now from a folded position, just as if you were a bulb, gradually start to unfold the different parts of the body using the exhalation of breath to move on. For example, the first part to move from this folded shape might be a clenched hand; take a deep breath and gradually, on the out breath, release the fingers. Next time perhaps the arms start to unfold, and so on

until you have stretched out the body into the position of a flower of your choice. Try to 'feel' that the body has become the flower; 'feel' the colour as well. Realise it is the breath which has given the impetus for growth.

4.   Travelling around the room quickly how you wish. When you hear the drum cue, stop and form yourself into the different stages of growth that a plant or flower goes through according to the seasons. So, for example, on the first drum cue it is spring and the bulb appears with shoots, travel again after you have formed a 'still' of that shape. On the second drum cue it is summer and full bloom, then autumn, etc.

5.   Now take a partner or four people work together. Create a movement sequence to this music of growth in whatever way you wish to interpret it. (Rehearse, perform, allow students to watch each other).

6.   Lie or sit and with closed eyes feel yourself to be as small as a pin. Listen to the silence in which a dropped pin could be heard. Now feel you are so large you cover the whole room. Now you are your own size. Be very aware of yourself and your size, in relation to the room. (Allow time for each direction).

7.   Standing, take one of the plants (try to bring large or spread-out plants; if you are unable to provide more than one or two, allow each student to perform separately). Hide yourself behind the plant and then let different parts of the body appear and move from behind the plant, as if they were offshoots. For example, a leg might slowly show itself and then hastily retreat; this can be a comic or serious improvisation. (*Music*)

8.   Perform a sketch where some of the students are flowers in a bed. The other student is a human, cuts the flowers and arranges them in a vase. Possibly the cut flowers droop, or have to be rearranged. Obviously the flowers have to move on their own to the vase, but then once in the vase the human will handle and place them as he wants. Make sure your face expresses how the flowers feel, i.e. relieved to be in water, fed up, dilapidated, etc.

9.   Create a sketch in groups of four or six where the plant is the focus of the piece. This does not have to be danced. You can use words, make a story, whatever you like, but the subject is the plant. (Rehearse and watch each other.)

10.   Listen to the music and move how you wish, but start

from an upward position and finish on the floor or chair or, if you are in a wheelchair, folded up.

11.   Lie or sit and relax. Talk through; relaxation. Let your whole body relax. You are lying on a bed of rose petals. The smell is wonderful. The bed is very soft, your face relaxes. Let all the tension go from the top of your head, the back of the neck, there is no strain across the chest, the shoulders drop, nothing to think about, just smell the rose petals and lie there, let your arms go, your hands and fingers. Let the back sink into the floor, the inside of your stomach relaxes. There is no tension in the legs or feet, everything sinks into the bed of rose petals. Just lie there, breathe deeply to smell the fragrance, just lie and relax.

Adult Workshop 12
Theme: Seaside
Time: 1½–2 hours

1.   Lie or sit and move each part of the body separately. Imagine that the body is submerged in warm water and that you are moving in isolation in the water. (*Slow music*)

2.   Now move the whole body together, still with the feeling that it is in water. Travel around the room as if floating, swimming, treading water, deep sea diving and exploring. Choose just one of these suggestions. (*Music*)

3.   Breathing stages 1, 2, 3 (see page 28).

4.   Choose an activity that could take place on the beach. For example, playing ball, making sand castles, looking for crabs, throwing stones into the sea. Now firstly perform a small sketch performing the activity as yourself. Then create a character to do this. Decide who you are – a child, an adult, what age, what shape; whether the character enjoys the activity, is good at it, is not really interested. When you have an image, repeat the sketch but add to it, for example, arriving at the beach, or perhaps the last game before it is time to leave, or perhaps pretending that it is too hot to go on playing, etc. The first time do this without music, the second time with the music.

5.   Take the movements of the activity you chose, i.e. digging and building, throwing and catching, searching and finding. Choreograph a dance sequence using these movements as well

as others, but the 'activity movements' are the theme of the dance. Do not enact any story, simply compose a dance sequence from the previous movements associated with your sketch. (*Music*) Tutor may need to demonstrate how such a composition could work.

6. Lying or sitting, just feel inwardly the following: lying on a rug, floating on your back, looking up at a blue sky; eating an ice cream cornet that is melting, pouring sand through your fingers and toes or someone else pouring sand over you, burying your face in the sand; wading into the sea which is cold; giant waves; sunbathing. (*Tutor call out*)

7. Now enact these sensations. (*Tutor directs*)

8. With a group of four people create a sequence where different characters are on a beach together. They do not necessarily know each other. For example, the tanning fanatic, the anti-social person who plays a transistor loudly, the sports, keep-fit addict. You can use words or not; although these characters are independent they react to each other.

9. With a group of two, four or six people, create a dance sequence which represents the joy of being at the seaside, the sense of freedom. Sometimes perform the dance at a normal tempo, sometimes in slow motion (like a TV replay). Occasionally some of the group are moving at one speed, whilst others at another. Rehearse this well. Allow students to watch each other's improvisations. (*Music*)

10. Travelling round the room how you wish, call out all the words that come spontaneously to you when you think of the seaside. Make gestures to give a colour to the words; for example you might want to shout out 'wonderful' and jump. Do whatever the word makes you want to. (*All at the same time*)

11. Lie and breathe gently. Relax to the music. (*Music*)

Adult Workshop 13
Theme: Abstract ideas taken from Picasso paintings. You can show cards of paintings from which you have taken improvisation subjects; I sometimes do.
Time: 2 hours. Allow a good time for each improvisation.
1. Lying on back on the floor (sitting if this is not possible), move each part of the body separately; then move the whole

body together. Repeat this on the stomach. If in chairs, turn the chair around to face a different way or sit facing the back of the chair. (*No music*)

2. Simple breathing exercises.

3. Travel around the room how you wish; as you move visualise that you are travelling in different ways. Maybe on a boat, swimming, flying like a bird, walking on air, floating; make movements that represent to you these different modes of travel. (*No music*)

4. Now will you imagine you are painting a portrait, of *yourself*. Draw yourself in the air. Then when you have drawn the outline stand in the pose you have drawn of yourself.

5. Take a partner. Look at each other (self-portraits, poses) and create a sequence of movements in the way that you feel your partner's self-portrait character would move.

6. Sit in a circle and feel inwardly as if you were a bird in a cage, a woman feeling very free and liberated, running on the beach, a couple dancing.

7. Enact and move as if you were the bird, the couple, the woman.

8. Take a partner and choose one of these subjects. Create a dance around it. Rehearse and then put it to the music (tutor has chosen appropriate music beforehand).

9. Together as a group make an improvisation where couples are dancing together. There is no need for everyone to have the same style of dance. Try to capture different personalities, characters, shapes and sizes. For example, elderly and jolly; bopping very cool disco, waltzing. It can be different nationalities. Decide which partner is male or female. You can change partners, but the male, if he changes, must take on the style of the next girl. Rehearse this and set it somewhere (maybe outside, in a ballroom, club, etc.).

10. Come back to floor or chair position that you started in and move slowly each part of the body, then let it relax until you are completely relaxed.

11. Relax (no talk through; just silence).

Adult Workshop 14
Theme: Abstract Ideas
Time: 1½–2 hours

Props: Cardboard boxes

1.   Lie on the floor (if not possible, sit in chair). Move each part of the body separately. Then move the whole body. Turn over and repeat on stomach. (*No music*)

2.   Simple breathing exercises.

3.   Travel around the room in a very neutral manner, disregarding people you pass. There is no feeling to the travelling, you are just moving. Now travel around the room shaking hands or touching other students. Each time you shake hands say, 'hello', in a different manner, i.e. loudly, softly, angrily, friendly, surprised, etc.

4.   Take some of the cardboard boxes and place them on parts of yourself (scissors are needed) so that you eventually create a character which is partly boxes. If it is possible, give this character a movement sequence to perform. If the boxes prevent you from travelling, make the characters move on the spot. (*Music*)

5.   Take a partner who is also a 'box person' and choreograph a dance story between the two characters. No words, just mime.

6.   Sit and feel inwardly: kind, gentle, shy, pushing.

7.   Move and interpret these different qualities.

8.   Take an object, any object (a book, a scarf, etc.) and handle it: as if it were a child, someone who you are not too keen on, two children playing together.

9.   Create a still life, a painting with yourself and any objects in the room you wish to use. In other words, arrange yourself and the objects to become a picture.

10.   Choreograph a group improvisation – no story just dance movements – using the boxes. (*Music*)

11.   Move how you wish to music (*disco or something with a good bouncing rhythm*). Let yourself really go and as soon as the music stops, immediately stand still. Become neutral, unaware of yourself or your surroundings.

12.   Lie or sit on the floor, relax each part of the body and breathe evenly in, out, in, out . . .

Adult Workshop 15
Theme: Acting exercises. Masks
Time: 2 hours

Purpose: Detailed attention to mannerisms, fun, projection.
Props: Masks

WARM-UP EXERCISES
1.   Standing, shake out all parts of the body. Shake out the whole body together. (*Music*)
2.   Stretch all parts of body. Stretch the whole body together. (*Music*)
3.   Circle the head, shoulders, elbows, arms, wrists, trunk, waist, hips, legs, ankles.
4.   Wriggle the fingers, toes, facial muscles, mouth, scalp.
5.   Relaxed, jump on the spot and travelling. (*Music*)
6.   Sitting, breathing exercises.
7.   Tighten then release all parts of the body separately. Tighten and release body as a whole. (*Drum accompaniment*)

OBSERVATION EXERCISES
These are exercises to recreate mannerisms you have observed in different people: walks, runs, sitting postures, smiles, facial expressions, etc.
8.   Recreate a real or imaginary person doing the following: peeling potatoes, picking flowers, making a bed, hanging clothes on the line, making a snowman without gloves on, taking a shower, making a salad.
9.   Perform the same actions as yourself.
10.   Now, as yourself, recall how you would react to the following: the smell of a rose, sucking a lemon, biting on something hard, something soft and chewy, taking a cold shower, a warm bubble bath, looking at a beautiful picture, looking up at a blue sky, remembering a past event.

MASK EXERCISES
11.   Realise that the face itself can become the mask. After performing the following exercises return the face to neutral. Remember that with mask work fluidity of the back is important also. To project to the audience, the head leads the way.
a.   From a neutral lying position, get up slowly, allowing the head to lead the way.
b.   Sitting in a circle, stretch the face into different mask positions. Return each time to neutral.

c.   Passing on exercises. Sitting on chairs side by side, 'pass on' the smile. The first student makes a small smile, the next person develops the smile, until by the time it reaches the sixth person it is a large grin. Pass the 'grin' down the line until it is again a small smile. Develop by 'passing on' expressions of anger, sorrow, etc.

d.   Standing, put on masks. Walk in different ways as before (see 8). Now use the character you were before (see 9). Make an entrance by opening a door and coming out into fresh air on a beautiful day. Now enter the house as if it were very cold outside.

e.   Develop: the character is having tea with an imaginary friend, gossiping, laughing, sipping tea and eating biscuits. (Rehearse this sketch. Pay particular attention to detail.)

f.   Masks on. Together with partner, mirror movements. One student is the reflection of the other. Suddenly the reflection refuses to reflect and begins to make independent movements. (*Background music*) This sketch can be very humorous.

12.   Group improvisation. Half the group wearing masks, half unmasked using own faces as masks. The unmasked students are puppets manipulated by the others. A story or dance sequence is choreographed from this beginning. (*Music*)

13.   Move as you feel when you hear the music. Work individually but interact with the group as a whole at the same time.

14.   Breathe gently. Lie and relax. On the drum cue sit up very aware of the past session.

Adult Workshop 16
Theme: Forbidden
Time: 2 hours
Purpose: To look at the idea of restriction from a theatrical and abstract angle. To be aware that confines do not necessarily mean restriction. Acceptance can, in most circumstances, result in enjoyment.

1.   Shake out to music, using all parts of the body (as described previously).

2.   Sitting, breathing exercises. Breathe as if the air was bad. Breathe as if you were by the sea.

3.   Lie on the floor and feel, with no outward expression, parts

of the body. Tutor directs: 'your centre, the ends of your body, your face, hands, feet, back of knees, back, toes, fingers, top of scalp, face; feel tight, relaxed, free.' (*Drum accompaniment*)

4.   Standing, perform any movements that give you pleasure.

5.   Travelling around the room, think of instances in everyday life where you are forbidden to do things. Assume the roles of two people; have conversations with the 'restrictor'. For example, 'Get off the grass', 'Oh, sorry, I didn't see the sign', 'You are not allowed to cycle through the park', 'Why not?' 'Don't push, go to the back of the queue', 'I was here first'. All the class speaks at the same time. The scenes can then be performed individually if tutor wishes.

6.   Develop this idea into movement. Perform everyday movements freely, suddenly become self-conscious and movements are restricted. (*Music*)

7.   Forbidden because of age. With a partner, think about stages of a human being's life: childhood, middle years, old age. Develop into a sketch to restrict another generation. For example: Parent to child: 'You cannot see that film, you are too young.' Child to parent: 'Mum, what are you dressed like that for? You can't go to a disco at your age.' Middle years to older generation: 'Now Gran, to waste your pension going to the Canary Islands is just plain daft.' Older person to middle years: 'You should not eat in the street, I was brought up never to eat in the street.' And so on. A very short dialogue continues with movements.

8.   React as you wish to the tutor's directions: 'Touch', 'Don't touch', 'Scratch', 'Stop scratching', 'Laugh', 'Stop laughing', 'Spread out', 'Take up less room'.

9.   Perform hand gestures which forbid, e.g. putting up hand to stop, shaking hand to say 'no', a gesture to indicate you wish to be left alone.

10.   Group improvisation (or two groups). A movement sequence where the dancers are linked together and therefore restricted in their movements. Gradually they break free and move with fluidity, ending dance sequence back in an inter-twined shape where there is fluidity of movement. (*Music*)

11.   Breathe gently. Sway from side to side, rock forwards and backwards, roll head, stretch arms, and sit quietly. (*Music*)

MIXED ADULT WORKSHOPS FOR ABLE AND DISABLED STUDENTS (DANCE UMBRELLA SERIES)

A series of workshops was given in London under the Dance Umbrella Festival. The purpose was to invite institutionalised students to work in different surroundings with dancers and to introduce interested dancers to the idea of working with these students. The series was very successful and everyone enjoyed themselves. A regular monthly dance club was organised as a result of the workshops.

Mixed Workshop 1

Professional dancers and physically disabled students.

Theme: Touch

Time: 2 hours

Some of the students were in chairs or on crutches. The degrees of handicap varied. When sitting, all students had chairs. With partner work, disabled students worked with dancers.

This workshop took place in an art gallery at ground floor level. The art gallery offered this space free, and the workshop took place before the gallery opened at noon.

1. Sitting in a circle call out your name and how you feel. (*Music*) Make a movement to show how you feel. Tutor demonstrates, for example: I hunch my shoulders because I am not sure how I feel.

2. Sitting or standing, warm up separately all parts of the body, i.e. move separately each part of the body. (*Music*)

3. Breathing exercises.

4. Touch yourself with another part of your body, i.e. knee can touch the back of the other knee, head can rub against the arm. If the disabled student is too limited in movement to do this, then work with a partner. (*Music*)

5. Massage any parts of your body that you feel are tense. Just gently rub or stroke those parts of the body. Work with a partner if it is not possible to do this yourself.

6. Make as many different dance movements as you can think of, holding on to a chair or object. For those who have little power in the arms, use paper fans, material, bean bags, elastic, etc. (*Music*)

7. Travel around the room feeling different surfaces and

textures. Notice the coldness of steel chairs, the texture of anything wooden, the texture of someone's clothing, etc.

8.   With your partner, make a sequence of movements where you have contact with each other. (*Music*)

9.   With eyes shut, feel inwardly the energy go to various parts of the body. 'Feel the top of your head, the tip of your nose, the back of your neck, your ankle bones, etc. Now inwardly feel, still with your eyes closed, that you are being pushed, pulled, stretched, crumpled up, rolled into a ball, flattened out.' (*Tutor directs with quiet drum accompaniment*)

10.   Take a new partner. One student shuts his eyes and touches and feels part of the other person (face, legs, hands, etc.). Now step away from your partner and try to recreate the movements and feeling you had when you were in contact with them. Change over roles and repeat.

11.   Tutor demonstrates simple routine done from chairs in twos. Students sit facing each other. An example routine could be:

a.   Sit forward and stretch arms out.

b.   Sit back and place hands on shoulders. Repeat. (The body will have a rocking movement of forward and back.)

c.   Stretch out one leg in the air and put it down.

d.   Stretch out the other leg in the air and put it down.

e.   Stamp one foot on the ground (knees bent).

f.   Stamp other foot on the ground (knees bent). Repeat c,d,e,f.

g.   Use your arms to make a climbing-a-rope movement above your head, four times, right arm, left arm, right, left.

h.   Then press both hands down to waist level either side of waist, palms down.

i.   Press up with hands, palms up, to just about face level. Repeat.

j.   Then with both arms, draw a large circle in the air and look at your partner while you are doing this.

Tutor demonstrates, students go through it without music, then when they have memorised it, perform the sequence to slow classical music developing their own personality of movement to the music (still using the routine).

12.   Play the students music of a different tempo (for example, jazz, reggae, Greek) and ask them to perform the same routine

facing a partner and therefore interacting with each other to this new music, bringing a new personality of movement to the same sequence. (Do not try to improvise dance sequences where partners touch each other when you have varying degrees of handicap. For example, saying clap hands together may be fine for those who have hands, but not for others.)

13.   Breathe gently.

14.   Relaxation; talk-through.

At various stages in this workshop ask students to show each other their work, individually or in pairs.

Mixed Workshop 2

Dancers, staff and mentally handicapped students.

Theme: Stretch

Time: 1½–2 hours

This workshop took place in a commercial dance studio (lent free of charge) where there were large mirrors all around the room and barres. The mentally handicapped students had come wearing tracksuits and therefore there were no problems about flexibility of movement because of unsuitable clothing. In this session some mentally handicapped students preferred to work together rather than with the other dancers; it was left to the students to choose. The age range was 14–25 years.

1.   Spread out in the room. Move each part of the body separately. (Tutor works alongside students.) (*Music*)

2.   In a circle, call out your name and make a movement to show how you feel about coming here today. (*Music*)

3.   Simple breathing exercises.

4.   Think of all the different ways you can stretch your body. Tutor demonstrates: 'You can stretch your hands like this or this, your arms . . . Now perform to the music many different ways of stretching.'

5.   Take a partner and do this with them. Stretching in different ways but holding on to each other or touching some part of the other person.

6.   Use the mirrors around the studio and use your reflection as your partner. Create stretching shapes with the reflection. (*Music*) (Some of the mentally handicapped students were fascinated by this and performed very exciting movements.)

7.   Move around the room quickly and lightly. When you hear

the drum beat, stretch up high and remain still. The second time move heavily and slowly. When you hear the maracas shaking, curl up into a ball on the floor.

8.   Lying on the floor, tense and relax separate parts of the body. (*Tutor directs. Drum cue*)

9.   Sitting up, feel inwardly without any outward expression: sleeping, anger, excitement. Now stand up and each time I beat the drum and call out a direction, mime the action: Lifting up something heavy; throwing up a ping pong ball; throwing a middle sized ball at a partner; throwing a very large ball at a partner. Now catching a ping pong ball, a middle sized ball, a very large ball.

10.   Walk round the room quickly. When I beat the tambour stop and call out as loudly as you can, 'Come on, you are late.' This time pretend you are chewing gum. After a time you pull it into different shapes. When you hear the drum beat, stop and call out, 'That is disgusting.' This part of the class created some very funny expressions.

11.   Finish with a simple routine taught by the tutor which can be done with a partner. (*Music*) Routine could be similar to the one described for the previous workshop. Students could perform sitting on the floor or standing facing each other.

12.   Breathing. Relaxation. Talk-through.

Mixed Workshop 3
Psychiatric patients and professional dancers.
Theme: Body Expression. Correction and distortion.
Time: 1½–2 hours

The session was held at a commercial dance studio. Dancers worked with patients during the partner work.

All students sat on chairs for exercises and work that would normally have been done on the floor. This was because some of the patients were quite elderly and all had come unsuitably dressed, i.e. tights, dresses, tight jeans, suits, etc. It is far more difficult to arrange proper clothing for this group of people because many of them will be discharged over a short period of time. However, with those who are resident, every effort should be made to ensure they have tracksuits or loose trousers to wear if they want to.

1.   Standing anywhere in the studio, move all parts of the body separately as you wish. Really 'feel' each movement, the first time move slowly. The second time move the body quickly but do not 'feel' the movement, just do it. Notice how the quality of movement is far less when you are unaware or do not 'feel' the movement. (*No music*)

2.   In a circle, call out your name and move to the rhythm of the music. (*Music*)

3.   Now, still moving to the rhythm, try to look at as many people's eyes as you are able to and nod or smile to them.

4.   Sitting, let us do breathing exercises. Stages 1, 2 (see page 28).

5.   Sitting without showing any outward expression or movement, direct all the feeling of energy to various parts of your body: your feet, stomach, legs, top of the head, bottom, back, etc. (*Tutor directs*)

6.   Travel around the room with this feeling of energy. This does not necessarily mean you have to move quickly. Perform any movements you like. For example, running, walking sideways, jumping, walking near to the ground, etc.

7.   Take a partner and perform a sequence of movements very slowly with a great energy behind the movement. Slowly, in the pace that Chinese or Indian dancers use. (*Music. May be Chinese music*)

8.   Sitting without showing it outwardly, feel as if you are sitting tensely, now relaxed. As if you are sitting badly, now your spine is straight and you are upright. Feel as if your face is tense, now relaxed. Your shoulders are hunched up because you are worried, now completely relaxed and well placed, etc. (*Tutor directs. Drum accompaniment*)

Now outwardly show these movements, correcting an incorrect posture. First time perform the movement incorrectly and the second time correctly.

9.   Massage parts of the body that you feel have tension. Take a partner and let your partner gently touch you wherever she feels there is tension. Change over. (*Music*)

10.   Now wrap your partner up as if she were a parcel. She is not wrapped up too well and no care is taken when handling her. The second time wrap your partner up with great care. (*Music*)

11.   Perform movements that you really enjoy. Maybe stretching, wriggling your toes; standing still and looking up at the sky. Just move in the way that gives you pleasure. (*Classical or jazz music, strong neutral sound, e.g. not a heavy beat so that there is no interpretation from the music – Bach, Vivaldi, Miles Davis, John Coltrane.*)

12.   Take a partner or by yourself just jam to the music (*disco or reggae etc.*)

13.   Make a circle. Call out your name and jump into a shape with your body that shows how you feel now. Hold the position until the next person moves.

14.   Sit in the chair, breathe gently and relax. (Talk-through then play very relaxing quiet music as the students rest.)

BEGINNING MOVEMENT SESSIONS FOR PSYCHIATRIC PATIENTS

Suggestions for the Tutor
As mentioned before, parts of all the previous adult workshops can be used with younger psychiatric patients, those students up to the age of 50 or 55. Most previous sessions are too long for these students. An hour class is enough. When planning movement improvisation for this group of people, know why you feel dance and creative movement can be beneficial. For psychiatric patients I particularly wish to focus on the following points:

1.   Fun.

2.   To allow people time to discover their own movement rhythm.

3.   For exercise and body control, and movement awareness.

4.   To have a clear framework which encourages fantasy, but has a discipline which enables the student to 'cut off' so that he is always in control, and the fantasy is not a means for self-indulgence.

5.   To encourage people to be less inhibited in movement and to socialise and work sensitively with the rest of the group.

6.   To encourage students to discover their full movement potential.

7.   Often students will prefer to sit on chairs in a circle rather than lie or sit on the floor.

I will reiterate certain suggestions for the tutor to bear in mind:

a.   Be flexible in your ability to change a planned session if, for some reason, the group does not respond well.

b.   Having established a 'theme' for the session, know what you hope to draw out from it.

c.   Sensitive timing is essential. Recognise instantly when the group is tired or the concentration is lost. Also, know how to stop any individual who may wish to talk or perform too long, and thereby tend to lose the interest of the rest of the group. This must be done in such a manner that the student does not in any way feel squashed.

d.   Never overstimulate or tire. The class should act as a stimulus but students should not feel 'wound up'.

e.   Participation must be voluntary, and the members of the class should be able to drop in, drop out, or just watch.

f.   Particularly for psychiatric patients, structure a class so that if some wish to do their 'own thing', for example, sing, read a poem, dance by themselves, it is possible at some point.

g.   Structure sessions which have parts almost like a disco (see following Method Classes).

h.   Choice of music is very important, a mixture of reggae, funk, lyrical, classical, jazz. Be careful when using electronic sounds as they can be disturbing for some people.

i.   Ensure that students are as relaxed as is possible. If the tutor sees someone making too much effort, he or she should ask them to pause, rest and start again when the body has relaxed.

j.   Plan part of the programme to include physical contact.

k.   Remember, in improvisation there is no 'right' or 'wrong' way. However, the quality of movement and projection are important and can be worked at.

l.   The tutor must be able quickly to communicate and relate his or her energy to the class. This does not, however, mean being 'hearty' or loud.

m.   Do not be 'thrown' by the lack of continuity of students who attend the session. Realise there will constantly be a change of people because of admissions and discharged patients.

n.   Never assume beforehand an individual's likely response to a dance session. From personal experience, the most unlikely students in appearance (e.g. very correctly dressed men wearing suits and shiny polished shoes, aged between 40–60) have turned out to be real 'swingers'.

o. Ensure the student feels 'safe' and never inadequate.

The following Method Class is one I would suggest as a structure around which ideas from previous adult work can be inserted.

Method Class 1
Time: 1 hour
Purpose: An introductory session which will encourage students to just 'move'. After such an introductory session, if the classes are to become a regular activity, 'themes' should be introduced (see Method Class 2).
1. Standing. Move all parts of the body as you wish. (Tutor demonstrates with class). Move your face, your neck, shoulders, head . . . (*Disco or similar music*)
2. Form a circle, join hands and rhythmically sway to music. Let go of hands and call out your name. (*Reggae or similar music*)
3. While we clap and move on the spot to music, each person call out how they feel at this moment: 'depressed', 'happy', and so forth.
4. Sitting (either on floor or if the group is timid or in middle years on chairs) in a circle. Breathing exercises first two stages only. (*Drum accompaniment*)
5. Standing, perform any stretch movements with your body that you can think of. (*Jazz music*)
6. Take a partner; keeping in contact with each other, perform stretching and reaching movements. You can stand, sit, lie side by side. Keep physical contact with some part of you. (*Music*)
7. Sitting in a circle (floor or chairs) and holding hands, sway to the music. Now one person gets up and goes into the middle of the circle to perform any movements he or she may like to do. Others clap to the rhythm. After a time, another person or two or three people go into the centre.
8. Standing, perform any dance movements that give you a

feeling of pleasure. (*Music*) Then join up with a partner and dance 'jazz' together. (*Jazz music*)

9.   Form a circle standing. Call out your names, one by one, and how you feel now. Call out as loudly as you can. Now call out in turn where you would really like to be at this moment, for example: 'by the sea', 'home' . . . (*Play music quietly as background impetus*)

10.   Break away from circle. Lie or sit and gently breathe. Relax.

Tutor: 'Thank you, I really enjoyed working with you. I hope you are not too tired.' If possible, allow time for students to come and talk to you if they wish to.

Method Class 2
Theme: Rhythm
Time: 1 hour
Purpose: To be aware of the 'feel' of movement. To recognise individual body rhythms. To work together as a group.

1.   Standing, warm up all parts of the body, moving as you wish. (*Tutor leads. Music*) Now when each part of the body is exercised, exercise the whole body together. It does not matter how the movements look at this stage, just get everything going together. (*Music*)

2.   Standing in a circle, clap to the music and make eye contact with as many of the group as you can. In other words, say 'hello' with your eyes. Call out your name when I point to you. When everyone has named themselves make a movement that you feel represents you and how you are feeling at this moment. (*Music*)

3.   Sitting in a circle on the floor or on chairs. Simple breathing. Inhale for four counts, hold for four counts, exhale for six counts, hold for four counts. (*Gentle drum accompaniment*)

4.   Tighten and relax each part of the body as I direct you. For example, clench the hands and fingers, release; clench the toes, release; tighten buttocks, let go. Now sit in a position that shows you are unrelaxed. How do you sit when you are anxious? Now sit in a position where you are completely relaxed and comfortable. Repeat this for standing, walking. Always correct the tension by easing out.

5.   Take a partner. Move how you wish but always have contact with your partner in the positions I give you: back to back, hands to hands sitting, side by side lying, head to head, toe to toe sitting . . . Tutor directs each couple into a different position. (*Music*) Then group watches individual couples. (*Classical music*)

6.   With the music, stretch and bend the body as you wish. Feel the sense of pleasure in stretching and then closing up. (*Music*)

7.   Sitting in a circle. One person stands in the centre and claps a rhythm. The rest of the group pick up the tempo and stamp it out with their feet. The person in the centre moves to the accompaniment. Change people in centre.

8.   Let us form a circle again as we began the session. Call out your name and make a movement of how you feel now. (*Music as background*)

9.   Lie or sit and breathe gently.

Method Class 3

Theme: Expression through body positions. Sense of travelling and stillness.

Time: 1 hour

Purpose: To show how the body can express words without the necessity for words. To show how different tempo of movement can indicate a sensation or emotion.

1.   Standing in a circle, call out your name. Follow this up by performing one fast and one slow movement. (*Music*)

2.   By yourself, move separately all parts of the body as you wish, very slowly. Really feel the movement. Now move the whole body together including facial muscles, fingers, toes, quickly. Catch the feel of that speed.

3.   Sit on chairs or lie on the floor, and without outward movement feel and direct all the energy to where I tell you (*Tutor directs*): your head, back of your neck, your toes, your cheeks, lips, legs . . . etc. Now feel without outward expression the following emotions: laughter in your bottom, scream with your feet, sorrow in your shoulders, surprise at the top of your head, peace in your arms.

4.   Standing, express in movement these same feelings as I direct you: peace in your walk, laughter in your face, sorrow in your hands, scream with your back.

5. Now let us take simple movements that can express how you feel. Be aware how the emotion influences the tempo you move at. Walk angrily, timidly, lazily, run with fear, with confidence, jump because you are startled, jump for joy, jump to avoid something, jump to catch something.

6. Take a partner. Imagine your partner is a parcel, wrap up the parcel in a hurried manner. Now wrap up the parcel so that all the paper is folded neatly. Change roles. (*Classical music*)

7. Travel around the room how you wish at varying speeds. When I give a drum cue stop and feel the stillness, be still. On the next drum cue move in physical contact with the person nearest to you. Move slowly and heavily. On the next drum cue remain still. On the third cue move lightly and travel with speed.

8. In a circle or wherever you wish to stand, dance to the music; if you feel like joining in with others, do so. (*Music: reggae, disco, jazz*)

9. Sitting in a circle, make eye contact with others in the group. When you catch someone's eye, hold his gaze and call out your names.

10. Breathe slowly and gently. Relax, shut your eyes, and recapture the feeling you had when you were still.

You will notice how these method classes have developed in content, yet the same form is kept. From these introductory sessions all the adult workshops previously written about can be introduced.

MOVEMENT FOR ELDERLY OR STROKE PATIENTS

Suggestions for the Tutor
The main reason why elderly people wish to participate in movement sessions is because they are anxious to keep their joints supple and tone up the parts of the body that are mobile. Stroke patients are motivated by the same reasons, but with this group of students it is important to encourage them constantly, as the very nature of their illness tends to make them feel depressed and enormous willpower is required in order that they don't give up.

Points I remind myself to think about when working with these groups are as follows:

1.   Always explain the reason why you are giving the session. If you simply present the class as 'music and movement' without an explanation of how it can be beneficial, the group can too easily feel that they are being treated like children. Explain each part of the programme as you go along.

2.   Always try to arrive in time to greet each member of the group individually.

3.   Remember that half an hour of concentrated movement can be as valuable as a longer session, during which the students may tire and lose their concentration.

4.   Choice of music is important. Classical, ethnic (such as Greek music), reggae, are all sounds that I have found were enjoyed.

The purposes of a movement session for the elderly are:

1.   To exercise in order to keep the body and joints supple.

2.   To co-ordinate movement and thought (see co-ordination exercises Method Class page 104).

3.   To keep the mind agile (see memory movement Method Class page 105).

4.   To communicate with each other and the tutor (see mime page 104).

5.   To be stimulated.

6.   To enjoy the movement, music and tutor.

All classes are taken sitting in a chair in a semi-circle, tutor in the front on a stool.

The following method class is written in detail. The class lasts approximately one half hour. I repeat the same class for each weekly session, occasionally changing the exercises and often changing the music.

Method Class 1
Time: ½ hour
Purpose: General toning up physically and mentally.

Suggested introduction: Hello. We are going to do our usual dance exercise session in order that you can get all the parts of the body working. Do whatever you feel able to. If anyone has a part of the body they wish to concentrate on, let me know at the end of session and I can give you some special exercises.

EXERCISES FOR THE ELDERLY

1. Gently shake out your head, shoulders, arms, hands, trunk, ankles, legs . . . (*Drum accompaniment*)

Now we will exercise from the head downwards. If one limb is not working, either use the paralysed limb like a pencil, pushing it with the arm or whatever, or improvise and use another part of you.

Sitting up in your chair as firmly as you can:

2. *Head Exercises*

a. Raise the head and chin towards the ceiling, then lower the head and chin to the chest. Return the head to the centre. Repeat three times. (*Drum accompaniment. Tutor demonstrates all the time*)

b. Incline the head one way and then the other. Return to the centre. Repeat three times.

c. Turn the head one way and then the other, and then roll it in a circle once right and then left.

3. *Shoulder Exercises*

a. Raise the shoulders up towards the ears and then drop downwards. Repeat three times.

b. Place your hands on your shoulders and circle your elbows towards the back. Repeat three times.

c. Now circle your shoulders backwards by themselves. Really feel the shoulder blades being pulled back as you do this. (Three times)

d. Pull your shoulders forwards and then to the centre. (Three times)

Pull shoulders backwards and then to centre. (Three times)

4. *Arm Exercise I*

a. Take your arms straight out in front of you, palms downwards.

b. Turn the palms up and raise your arms until they are above your head.

c. Look up so that the whole body is stretched up.

d. Lower your arms downwards in front of you with your fingers moving at the same time. When the arms reach shoulder level, bring the hands to the shoulders and then lower the arms to your side.

5. *Arm Exercise II*

a. Take your arms out in front of you and clasp hands.

b. With your hands clasped strongly together bring both hands to your chest, elbows to the side.

c. Still with clasped hands, straighten arms in front of you.

d. Raise your arms, hands clasped, above your head. Do not look up.

e. Bring arms down to chest level, unclasp hands and relax arms to sides. (Repeat three times)

6. *Arm Exercise III*

a. Draw a large circle in the air with each arm.

b. Draw a large circle with both arms together.

7. *Arm Exercise IV* (*climbing a rope above you*)

a. Use your muscles to pull on the rope.

b. Take the same idea of 'pulling in' something to either side of you.

c. Now push out with one arm while at the same time pulling in with the other (good for co-ordination).

8. *Arm Exercise V*

a. Cross over the arms, hands on opposite shoulders.

b. Release the hands and take the arms out in front of you.

c. Repeat a. and b. three times.

d. Raise the arms up in front of you crossed over until they are above your head.

e. Uncross them and bring them down to the sides of the body. The movement is like describing a circle in the air.

9. *Arm Exercise VI*

a. Arms out in front of you, palms facing downwards.

b. With the arms still out, turn the palms upwards.

c. Arms out, turn palms downwards again.

d. Clench the hands into a 'fist' and squeeze so that the arm muscles are strengthened.

e. Still clenching the fist, turn the fist upwards (in the same way as the palms were turned) and bring the clenched hands to rest on the shoulders.

f. Release the hands and arms to unfold and move downwards until they rest by your side.

10. *Trunk Exercises* (*to stretch the trunk*)

a. Stretch forward in your chair with your arms outstretched. Pull in something heavy and imaginary towards your stomach. As you pull in, make sure your stomach and buttock muscles are really working. (Repeat three times)

b. Sitting straight in your chair, stretch down with one arm to the side of your chair. The body is stretching sideways but facing front. Pull up something imaginary. Repeat to the other side of the chair. (Repeat each side two times)

c. Holding the side of your chair, arch backwards as if you are looking up to the sun, then round the back and gently lower the head towards the knees. (Once only)

d. With the hands on the waist, twist the waist to one side and then the other. Repeat twice.

e. In the chair, rock forwards and backwards. Repeat a number of times.

f. Sway sideways with body and arms.

g. Round the back and tuck the chin onto the chest. Begin to straighten the spine vertebra by vertebra. The head comes up last of all.

11. *Finger Exercises (older people are anxious to exercise the hands in order to keep them supple. Many different combinations of hand movements can be improvised)*

a. Use the fingers as if playing the piano.

b. Clench the hands and fingers and release.

c. Rub the hands together washing the hands, twisting the hands in all directions.

d. Put the heels of the hands together, centre of the hands, tips of the fingers, release and put backs of the hands together. (Repeat three times)

e. Circle the wrists. Pedal the wrists up and down.

f. Shake the hands and wrists until they are quite relaxed.

g. Use the hands as if they are waves in the sea. Let the hands undulate.

12. *Hand Exercise I*

a. Clenching the hands in a fist shape, release the little finger, the next finger, the middle finger, the forefinger, the thumb.

b. Splay the hands out.

c. Close in the thumb, forefinger, middle finger, next finger, little finger. You have a 'fist' shape again.

d. Repeat.

13. *Hand Exercise II*

a. Intertwine the fingers of the two hands together and push the heels of the hands against each other, so that the elbows are pushed out sideways.

b. Still with hands locked, push the arms out to a straight position in front of you.

c. Release and let the arms fall to the sides of the body completely relaxed.

14. *Leg Exercises (Improvise with combinations of leg movements that tone up calf and thigh muscles)*

a. Stretch the leg out in front of you off the ground.

b. Flex the ankle up towards you, stretch the foot downward, repeat with leg outstretched. Flex, stretch, flex, stretch. Repeat with other leg.

c. Raise both legs in the air, ankles flexed towards you, arms stretched out. Note how the stomach muscles have to work when doing that.

d. Sitting in the chair, do a walking movement with the legs. Co-ordinate by swinging opposite arm forward to the leg. *(Tutor demonstrates and says 'walk and walk . . .')*

e. Cross the legs over one way and then the other.

f. Lift both legs off the ground, knees bent.

g. Draw circles in the air with alternative legs. This can be developed into drawing letters of the alphabet or numbers in the air.

15. *Feet and Ankle Exercises*

a. Circle ankles one way and then the other (repeat three times each).

b. Heels on the floor, balls of the feet on the floor (repeat three times).

c. Heels together, toes together. Feet parallel.

d. Pedal your feet up and down keeping contact with the floor, ball, heel, ball, heel.

16. *Co-ordination Exercises*

a. Curl up the toes and stretch out the fingers. Reverse. Clench the fingers and stretch out toes.

b. One hand behind the back, one hand on top of the head. Reverse.

c. Drop the head down and flex the ankles. Reverse.

You can think up many different movements for co-ordination based on ideas like this.

17. *Mime Exercises*

a. Describe with your hands the first thing you would like to do when you leave hospital and go home. For example, would you switch on the TV, make a cup of tea, switch on the radio? (In my experience, elderly people have very much enjoyed describing their pleasures and often it has resulted in the group getting into conversation with each other.)

b. Describe with your hands the work you did before you retired. (Again, a very much enjoyed exercise. It is also fascinating for the tutor to see the very different backgrounds all these students come from.)

c. Describe with your hands your favourite hobby.

d. Shut your eyes and feel this object (perhaps a balloon, a flower vase, crumpled paper, etc.). Now take the object away and ask the students to recreate the shape and feeling they had when they were handling the object.

18. *Rhythm*

I will clap a rhythm. Please can you repeat the rhythm. If you do not have the use of one arm, clap the rhythm on your knee or chair, or use your feet.

Although these exercises have been written in detail, they take a very short part of a session. It is important for the tutor to demonstrate them well. These exercises are performed at the beginning of the session without music in order that the students feel the movement. At the end, repeat to music.

There are many exercises you can devise which strengthen the muscles but do not strain the body. All these sessions are taken sitting in chairs in a circle.

Method Class 2
Time: ½–¾ hour
Purpose: General toning up physically, for mental and physical stimulus.
1. Exercises as explained.
2. *Memory Movement Exercise.* Tutor says 'I am going to perform three different movements with my hands. Do not copy the movements while I perform them, but memorise them. Then you repeat them from memory. This is the first movement, raising my hand. This is the second movement, turning my head. This is the third movement, drop your hand. And so forth. Mr X, can you give us three different movements with your hands, and afterwards we will repeat them.' This has

always been a favourite part of the sessions I have given, as older people are anxious to stimulate their memories.

3. *Letters and Numbers in the Air Exercise.* The purpose is for concentration and control of movement. One person thinks of a number or letter and draws it clearly in the air. Anyone in the group calls out if they recognise the letter. This can be developed into writing three-letter words and Christian names. The legs can also be used to trace out letters.

4. *Co-ordination Exercises.* Tutor improvises with any movements that require co-ordination. For example, circle the wrist and ankle, stretch one leg and bend one arm, drop the head and lift the arms, stretch out the arms and bend the legs . . .

5. *Movement Routine (1)* Compose a simple routine (sequence of movements that the group can learn and perform to music). Here is an example for a group in chairs: stamp and clap to one side, then to the other, rock forwards, backwards, forwards, backwards; rope climbing movement four times; stamp four times. (The length of sequences can be increased each session.) There are many routines that can be performed from wheelchairs that include combinations of exercises. Most elderly people I have worked with enjoy moving to lively music such as reggae or Greek music when it comes to this part.

6. *Movement Routine (2)*:

   a. Cross the arms to opposite shoulders.
   b. Release the arms down to sides of the body.
   c. Repeat a. and b.
   d. Swing arms right, left, right, left, body swaying.
   e. Stretch out the right leg in front of you.
   f. Stretch out the left leg in front of you.
   g. Bend the knees and put both heels on floor, feet upwards.
   h. Both feet onto the balls of the feet, heels in the air. Repeat.
   i. Finish by lifting arms into the air and drawing a large circle and relaxing hands to the body sides. Repeat.

7. Return to the original exercises, but this time perform to music.

8. Finish with gentle breathing exercises.

   I never say use your right or left arm or leg as this will muddle a class, some of whom may only have partial use of the body. Therefore I would suggest that the direction is thus:

'Swing one way and then the other. Stamp one foot and then the other.' Your own demonstration will help the group to follow.

During the routine section see if the group can remember the movements after a time. Then all you need to do is call out the directions. The first few times you will need to demonstrate. Choose music that the group responds to.

BEGINNING MOVEMENT SESSIONS WITH MENTALLY DISABLED PEOPLE

Introduction

My sessions have been with young and older adults, adolescents, and younger mentally handicapped students. I describe the method sessions that I have used with them. Their sense of fun, rhythm and supple bodies make exciting material for creative movement.

1. It is important to enhance their awareness of space.
2. To help them have control over their movements.
3. To develop their powers of concentration.
4. To recognise that within the adolescent with Down's syndrome, regardless of his rated intelligence, there is an adult part who wishes to express movement in the same way as any other young person, to disco dance or whatever the current trend is at that time.
5. To encourage the drama side.
6. To work on the quality of movement as with any other group.

Many of the suggested ideas written in the children's 7–10 section can be used within the suggested framework of the following Method Class. This class lasts a little over an hour and would need to be divided into two parts.

Method Class

Theme: Getting to know the body; awareness of space
Time: 1 hour
Purpose: As above

1. Standing in a circle, clap to the music. Join hands, move around in a circle one way and then the other. (*Music: reggae or good disco beat*)

2.   Take a partner, touch each other as the tutor directs; head, palms, backs of hands, elbows, back to back . . .

3.   Sitting down, simple breathing exercises: inhalation and exhalation.

4.   Sitting, move different parts of the body as tutor directs: pull in stomach, wriggle toes and fingers, push out chest, make faces, tighten bottom.

5.   Develop this by feeling imaginary situations: prickly, cold, hot sweaty, cool stiff, loose. Students perform these sensations.

6.   Travelling around the room as the tutor directs: arms in front, arms to side, arms behind; travel backwards, forwards, sideways, on toes, stretch high as you move; walk on flat feet near to the ground; move in circles, in straight lines, zigzag; walk on heels, feet turned out, feet turned in; run with head down, run with head up and arms behind you.

7.   Cover as much of the room as you can with large steps. Make yourself as wide as possible. Take small steps and become thin and small. Flatten yourself against the wall so that you become part of the wall. Flatten yourself against a partner. Flatten yourself so that you are part of the floor. Make the body into angles and corner shapes. Now make the body into round or curved shapes. (*Tutor directs; drum*)

8.   Make movements that show how you feel. If you feel angry dance angrily; if you feel gentle then move with that feeling; happy, sorrowful, excited, quiet movements. (*Tutor directs; drum*)

9.   Memory Movement. One person makes a movement. The next student has to remember that movement, copy it, and then add on a new movement, so that students make a 'movement chain'. Do this in groups of four and try to see if four chain movements can be memorised.

10.   Move as you wish but use stamps, high claps in the air, rubbing hands together, walking backwards, holding someone's waist, linking arms, eyes shut, arms out so that you do not bump into anyone. (*Tutor directs; music*)

11.   Now I will play some reggae and jazz. Dance how you wish with other people or by yourself.

12.   Sitting in a circle, breathe gently with your eyes shut. Now listen to this classical music and just enjoy the sounds.

Further Suggestions for Future Classes

(Remember many of the ideas from the children's or adult section can be used.)

1. Improvisation with props such as chairs, balls, material, hats.

2. *Use of chalk*. Let students draw shapes and then form the body to resemble the shape drawn. (To the tutor the two may not appear to correspond; this is not important, for it must be the student's translation.)

3. *Newspaper*. Let the student improvise by tearing, scrumpling and throwing the paper. Then ask the student to act out what he has just done. Using coloured chalk or paper, draw different areas of colour on the floor. Ask students to place themselves in a specific colour when the music stops.

4. *Games of balance*. For example, freezing in a given position and not wobbling. Change and let students wobble and deliberately lose their balance.

5. Some students make their own music with percussion instruments while the others move to these sounds.

6. Enact stories and everyday situations which happen to them.

7. Students teaching 'Keep Fit'. Students make up their own exercises and teach them to the rest of the group as well as to the tutor.

8. Students choose their music for parts of some sessions and bring tapes and records.

9. Take students to see professional dance performances.

10. *Observation*. Allow students to mime characters they encounter every day. Ensure they pay attention to details of mannerisms. For example, if a bus conductor or driver, help them to recall all the working movements that such a person would do.

11. Encourage students to listen and really hear many different countries in music and recognise the rhythms, such as Asian music, eastern, African, western, Greek, Russian, etc.

12. Remember that despite the assessed mental age of such students, adolescents and adults respond to rhythm and dance in the same manner as the rest of us. They wish to dance socially, disco, soul, whatever is the current fashion and some part of a session should provide time for this.

POINTS TO REMEMBER FOR THOSE WORKING WITH PARTIALLY SIGHTED OR UNSIGHTED STUDENTS

All the previous workshops are suitable for these students.

1. Some younger students have very little point of reference when discovering a movement vocabulary. For example, one unsighted eight-year old child I worked with had to be shown the movement feeling for words such as 'stretch', 'swing', 'bend', 'curl'.

2. Much attention should be focused on students' awareness of space.

3. Often it is a good idea to start the class in a circle holding hands so that everyone feels the circle shape. Move around together in the circle one way and then the other. One student can then weave in and out of the circle touching his colleagues as he travels.

4. Balance of the body again needs to be worked on. Many simple exercises for balance can be worked on. For example:

Run. Stop. Stretch up on toes and remain still.

Holding on to a partner make a series of balanced positions on one leg, kneeling, sitting on different parts of the body.

Balanced positions holding on to a chair or bar. Then letting go and trying to hold on to the position.

Balanced positions with partners. Back to back, side to side, palm to palm, kneeling facing each other.

Spin, stretch up and stand quite still, your body centred so that there is no wobbling.

Tutors can improvise many such combinations of movements and so can the students.

It is essential that these students wear flexible clothes, and have either bare feet or soft dance or PE shoes.

5. Improvisation with objects. Objects that have solid surfaces to touch, such as chairs, balls, boxes, etc. The paper tearing game described on page 78 can be adapted so that the students translate the sound of tearing or handling the paper into a movement.

6. Use of water to indicate the choreography of a floor pattern or movement shape. If a student wishes another to move in a certain direction or shape, they can dip their fingers in a bowl of water and trace the pattern on the forehead or arm of the other student.

7.   Have as many percussion instruments as possible so that students can compose their own sounds.

8.   Put emphasis on working together physically in order that students become sensitive to the rhythm and timing of each other.

9.   Touching objects and recreating the shape and feel of them.

10.   Touching each other and recreating the shape and feel.

11.   Repetition of floor patterns so that they can 'feel' space for choreographing movements.

These are only extra suggestions. All the previous method classes are in most parts suitable for unsighted students.

DEAF STUDENTS

Most of the previous workshops are suitable for these students, provided the tutor has an interpreter or a knowledge of sign language. Obviously it is not possible to ask students to perform lying down movements unless they are absolutely clear about instructions before hand. Music can be used, wooden floors transmit vibrations and rhythms can be picked up from observation rather than hearing. A drum is very good, as the action can indicate when to start and when to stop. I feel dance movement for these students is a very important part of their learning.

3: THE FORMATION OF SHAPE

In Chapter One I described how my creative movement classes with handicapped children developed and expanded into a multi-arts organisation for people of all ages and conditions. This chapter takes up the story at the point where our grant from the Leverhulme Trust came to an end. I hope that it will show how valuable all the creative arts can be in enriching the lives of handicapped and deprived people in the community.

There had been no time to consider what our next step would be when the grant money came to an end, but, as had happened a number of times before, at exactly the right moment another door opened. I received a telephone call inviting me to meet the Director of the UK Gulbenkian Foundation. At our meeting he said he had heard about the team's work and confessed to being somewhat bewildered by the number of individuals or arts organisations who were now carrying out similar work. We both agreed that the problem was to prevent overlapping and fragmentation, which was not healthy if the arts were to be seriously considered for their healing potential. The Director said, 'Perhaps you would like to go away and think out a way of consolidating and co-ordinating the overall picture.'

As I walked away from the Gulbenkian offices, an idea began to evolve, and at the end of the week I returned with a proposal. A free agency could be founded that would introduce the performing arts and professional artists of all disciplines to creatively deprived pockets of the community. The artist and performer would be paid for their services. The agency would provide regular creative activities and entertainments wherever needed. The individual institutions would contribute however much they could afford towards a performance fee, the project subsidising the rest. My hope was that such a clearing house, open to all sides, would prevent some of the isolation that confused many of us.

I was told that before the application could be considered I must secure office accommodation. How do you find this if you have no concrete guarantee of being able to pay for it? I scoured the city centre with the, by then rather tatty, Gulbenkian application. It reminded me of the days of 'Ariadne and the Golden Thread' in Richmond Gardens.

Eventually the thread led to an extremely successful business-woman who rented out offices in Covent Garden. She was a person who had a strong sense of social responsibility. Often, if she liked a scheme that would help the community, she reduced the rent. My first meeting with her was alarming. She wore huge dark glasses. I had been told by a friend to get the whole idea out in under five minutes because her time was precious. I took a deep breath. She liked the proposal. 'Do you really expect me to keep the space vacant while the Gulbenkian Foundation makes up its mind?' she asked. With another deep breath I assured her it was only a formality. 'What are you going to call the project?' she asked. Driving home, I thought, what words do I enjoy the sound of, and what is the project trying to do? Ideas only work if there is a form to them, and Shape is a good sound. Three months later Shape was installed in Covent Garden.

The number of 'back in an hour' notes pinned to Shape's door during the next few weeks would have covered a wall. An advertisement for an assistant brought a folk singer who had also had public relations experience. Heather was looking for a challenge and she felt she had found one in Shape. Together we set up an administration. Heather designed the letterheadings. Posters were distributed to hospitals, prisons and theatres. Endless letters went out to other arts organisations telling them of our existence. We had many rebuffs from these organisa-tions, who felt we would not last more than a few months.

Gradually artists of all skills began to drift in. We realised that it was essential to get them work quickly, otherwise the word would pass around that Shape was all ideas and no action. Heather and I had competitions as to how many hospitals we could persuade to make use of our artists. Then I hit upon the method that helped to make Shape so quickly successful. Why should an institution commit time and energy to finding a means of paying for a hitherto untried activity, particularly since there were no funds within their own budgets? We introduced a three months free trial period, during which the project paid the artists' hourly fees. With this approach, we were quickly able to link the two sides together. It was all-important to see the work of the artist before making an introduction. The practical experience of my previous work helped when fitting the right personality to the client. Heather acquainted herself with all the areas we hoped to service and she soon became sensitive and intuitive to marrying up the two sides.

At this time most of our work was being done in hospitals. Strangely, from the outset, the register of artists became international: English, Scottish, Israeli, Italian, West Indian, South American, Polish, American, African, Asian. Some had worked in similar places within their own countries. They did not join because it was a way of earning a living, for the most we were able to offer at that time was two hours work a week. They were genuinely interested in the concept of widening the area of people with whom they could communicate. Although the technique of a skill may be universal, working in different environments and having different cultural backgrounds can make the presentation of a creative discipline exciting.

There should be many more opportunities for the inter-national interchange of artists. In every walk of life a less parochial outlook would be achieved if government agencies organised swap-overs to encourage a wider experience.

Performing groups during the first few months did not appear as readily as single artists. We spent many happy evenings in pubs listening to bands and inviting suitable groups to perform. Once it was known we paid reasonable fees, the performers also began to contact us. One morning an African wearing a crown swept in. 'My name is Lord Eric,' he declared, 'and I would like to take my soul brothers into borstals to play.' I went to hear the soul brothers one Sunday afternoon. Despite one or two mishaps, when the fire-eater slipped on the paraffin and broke the saucer balancing the candle perched on his forehead, the entertainment was magical for the children watching. Heather telephoned a borstal and suggested an ethnic musical evening. The governor agreed enthusiastically. He had a number of West Indian youths in the centre. Lord Eric arrived with his group and their African instruments. When they made their first appearance of the evening the audience roared with laughter at Eric's crown. I thought the show was lost. After ten minutes, like the children on the Sunday afternoon, they were completely absorbed by the music. Eric decided to go the whole way. He told them African Anansi stories. These are comparable to Aesop's fables. Had it not been for his personality they would perhaps not have received the stories with such silent attention. The finale came when some boys played the instruments and others danced spontaneously in the aisles. Even the stern faces of the warders relaxed in the warm atmosphere. Watching, I realised how far entertainment can go towards helping break down barriers of communication.

It was important that every group should receive a proper fee, because we wished to put our audiences on the same footing as other audiences, in this way preventing any attitudes of patronage. Puppeteers, dancers, fringe theatre groups, music hall artists, magicians, classical musicians, folk singers, jazz players, all volunteered to put their names on our register. It was fun going to watch rehearsals or to see them perform.

Six months later Heather left to continue her folksinging career in America. An exciting new colleague arrived. Helen Poyner had applied for the post of assistant when I first advertised. She told me about her theatre background and the work she was doing in halfway houses. The maturity of this young person of 23 was unusual. She looked about 15 or 16. I told her when she applied for the job initially that she looked so young it could be a problem in setting up a new organisation. But when Heather decided to leave I rang Helen on the offchance that she might still be interested. That very day she had given in her notice. 'I still look 15,' she said. 'Never mind, I make up for both of us now,' I replied. So began a fruitful and happy partnership.

How We Worked

It was difficult to run the administration, travel to meet staff within their own environment, as well as watch new groups perform. We began to ask solo performers to come to the tiny room at Covent Garden. If they could survive that, they could survive anything. Our landlady occasionally poked her head around the door to see a mime, a folk singer or a magician giving us a sample of their talents. Visual artists always brought slides. Poets gave readings while all this was going on. Meanwhile the phone rang constantly and had to be answered. Slides and samples of work festooned the office floor.

Somehow we managed, in a very unorthodox and, to outward appearances, utterly chaotic way, to be extremely efficient. In four years there were only two times when performers were criticised. Amazingly there were no complaints about those artists who gave regular weekly workshop sessions. The gruelling task of raising money took up a considerable part of each day. We relied entirely on charitable money to keep the project alive. Neither of us knew any of the right people. Each letter had to be written and slanted differently. The size of the fund-raising file grew and grew. The Arts Council and the DHSS welcomed the idea, but wanted proof that such a service was needed and would not collapse. We literally lived from month to month during the first two years. Only Helen and I knew how often Shape was near to collapse. From outward appearances, here was an organisation acting like a hip mini Arts Council, subsidising workshops and performances as if money were not a problem. Somehow most worthwhile projects always do manage to survive, but the mental exhaustion and anxiety are a high price to pay for those who take the responsibility for such projects. Industry should be encouraged to investigate the potential of small charitable schemes which need financial support. Perhaps industry could adopt a few such schemes and allow the projects not only to have some material help but also the expertise of their business acumen in running an efficient administration. In return the projects should keep their sponsors fully informed of all developments, with an open invitation to drop by at any time.

There was one encounter we had that seemed like a fairy story. One foundation referred to Shape the secretary of another trust who was investigating the arts and disability. We supplied him with all the information we could. At the end of the afternoon he asked if we had any financial problems. 'No, we are fine at present, we have enough to last us at least six months,' I said. This kindly man looked somewhat taken aback. 'Well, if you do, put in an application to my Trust. I am sure it would be seriously considered.' Helen and I stared at him. 'You mean, you came to offer us money!' she said. In our limited experience no one had ever approached us with such an invitation. That particular trust helped to develop Shape services from then on.

The Artists' Work

On visits to many institutions, I was depressed by the blank walls that stared back at the waiting people. Inspired by Peter Senior, a visual artist who had organised the interior decoration for a group of Manchester Hospitals, we arranged for artists to paint murals in a hospital specialising in the treatment of cancer and in a children's ward. The general response was so enthusiastic that we applied to the Manpower Services Commission for a scheme that would enable an artist to work with unemployed people and a team of workers to spend one year decorating two hospitals in the East End of London. These were old Victorian buildings which needed large murals. By the end of the year, Michele, an Italian artist, produced with his helpers an exciting and vivid decoration. Hospital administration took a keen interest in such projects from the outset. They passed the designs only after a number of sketches had been submitted to them. Regular patients and staff watched the scheme from the time of rubbing down the walls and making good, until the opening view of the completed works. It was a fascinating opportunity for the viewers to see the process and stages of the artist's work. For the painter, who often works in isolation, it was a new experience.

Long after the works were finished, I visited the out-patients' departments to ask staff and the public for their response. The decoration had promoted a feeling of stimulus. There were those who liked the subject matter, and others who suggested they would have preferred a different composition. Everyone had observed and thought carefully about the murals. A painting of Whitechapel market, which was on the opposite side of the road to the hospital, was of concern to a woman patient who lived locally. She pointed out that since

Michele had begun his work the prices of fruit and vegetables had changed. She suggested he should come in regularly to repaint the labels at the current rate. Comments of this nature would rarely happen in a formal setting. Staff were equally interested and responsive. It must always be remembered by the artist/performer that it is as important to bring pleasure to those caring for disabled people as well, for the staff spend three-quarters of their time in the same environment. There were also schemes for patients or prison inmates to decorate their surroundings.

Michele went on to run his own decoration schemes. At the time of writing, he is designing a garden for the handicapped in a way that will allow them to tend it for themselves. Another garden idea was less fortunate. A sculptor and his wife had reclaimed a piece of waste land next to an old people's hospital and made a country cottage garden. Hollyhocks, sunflowers and stock stood up valiantly to the fumes of the passing juggernauts. Unfortunately the old people were prevented from enjoying the garden because vandals threw broken glass and cans over the high wall. This was something no one had anticipated.

It would be pleasing to see similar decorative projects financed by Manpower Services for brightening up the bleak walls of such places as Social Security offices, where long queues of unemployed have to wait. Subways and many other grey areas of building also cry out for colour.

My visit to Hospital Audiences Inc., a similar organistion to Shape in New York, as well as to a number of community arts projects, gave me many new ideas and recharged the initial focus that had recently tended to become swamped by paperwork.

Back in London, our agency was beginning to be used by many more disadvantaged pockets of the open community: centres for the homeless, self-help groups, youth groups, Salvation Army Day Centres, to mention just a few. Setting up a steel band group for young blind players after their everyday work was one such venture which also involved the cooperation of the local authority. They provided transport to collect the students. We organised pans to be made with the keys slightly raised for touch. This weekly event was useful and enjoyable in many ways for these young people. Apart from teaching them a skill, it enabled them to socialise with each other. One of my favourite outings was to sit and listen to the band. Later when they became more professional they played in hospitals and centres.

Woolfgang Stange, who had stayed on and developed his work since the early Leverhulme days, began teaching modern dance to another unsighted group of students on the other side of London. His triumph was when one totally blind dancer became accomplished enough to choreograph for the rest of the dancers. Woolfgang's work with the mentally handicapped was exceptional. On my first visit to the institution I was shown the patients with whom he was to work. Some were strapped to chairs. The staff warned him not to expect too much. Four years later, these same patients were able to perform with the blind and professional dancers in a show during which they were on stage for an hour. Again, half the value and fun was in being able to mix with other people outside their usual surroundings. Wherever possible activities such as these should take place within their usual venues, in order that isolated groups of people can go out to be entertained or to participate, becoming part of the everyday public.

As a result of a jazz performance in a borstal, another steel band was set up. This activity became so popular that they now have two bands. Poetry, folk, music hall, classical music and dance groups entertained in every possible place. We learnt much from the comments and suggestions of the audiences. A poetry and folk performance was welcomed but criticised by the inmates of a prison. The singer made the mistake of singing a number of songs about problems and political views that the men might have experienced. They explained to her, 'You don't need to tell us about our problems. We face them all day.' but by no means did they always wish merely for light entertainment.

Performers enjoyed entertaining to unusual audiences. They all felt that there was much to be gained from people in these situations. Audiences are less inhibited; they like to communicate with the artists after the show, asking questions about their lives and training, and making suggestions about what appeals to them. For the performer there is the challenge of having to captivate the audience in the first few minutes. A live show is an unaccustomed event. No one pays for a ticket, which makes it easier for someone to walk out at any time. Once the artist has made contact, the concentration and enjoyment during a show are completely wholehearted.

Particular occasions have photographed themselves on my memory. There was the African conga drummer frantically returning the salutes of an expatriate Polish patient in a psychiatric hospital. This man stood up in front, standing stiffly to attention and saluting time and again to show his appreciation. He wore his old uniform, including the cap. Jimmy drummed with one hand and saluted with the other. 'Wow, that was spaced out, man, that was in the clouds,' said the bandleader as we packed up. I remember the faces of the children in hospital watching an imaginary big dipper, when a visiting American theatre group created a fairground for them. There was the love and nostalgia radiating from an alcoholic woman as the saxophonist played her request tune. There was the touring company of the Royal Ballet getting ready for a show with such care it might have been a first night at Covent Garden. There was the pain that came out in women's poems written while they were serving a sentence. Puppeteers, clowns, poets, singers, magicians, all these images are associated in my memory with wide smiles and shiny eyes. Often an entertainment would provide the motivation for a regular weekly activity. From a poetry reading, a regular writing group grew. A one-act play and a mime show drew the interest of some homeless young people who had ended up in the West End of London with little to do and nowhere to live. They asked for a drama improvisation class.

Good will came from all sides towards Shape's activities, yet often I was asked, 'Isn't this just icing on the cake?' Yes, of course, in many ways a service such as this is only providing small amounts of icing, but if it creates a more palatable coating, then it achieves a result. This well-meaning question is indicative of the attitude towards socially disadvantaged people. Nobody questions you or me as to whether an evening at the pictures is just icing on our lives. Such remarks indicate a selective attitude to the direction of the performing arts and would seem to exclude a large proportion of the community. There is a need for new attitudes and policies which might eventually preclude the need for a service like Shape.

Workshops

Regular weekly workshops formed a large part of the programme. When looking at our application for charitable status, the commission enquired about the definition of the term 'workshop'. Was it a place where a number of persons made garments in a small working area? I think the misuse of the term began when it was used to replace the word 'class'. To encourage people to participate but not necessarily learn a technique, the word 'workshop' was introduced because it sounded less formal.

My first introduction to 'dossers' was when I went to a day centre in Covent Garden. The organiser showed me around this old building and introduced me to some of the men. Here was a group of people who had dropped out of the mainstream, either by choice or circumstance. They were independent free spirits who looked on life with humour. This centre was run by understanding Methodists. There were few rules; 'No bottles' was the most strictly enforced. The director decided to try out wire sculpting sessions and music/singing. Raphael, a talented Israeli artist who was achieving remarkable results in a centre for problem drinkers, was chosen for the sculpting. Bridget, a beautiful actress, gave the music sessions. Both of them found it took a little while to hit the right note and gain the confidence of the men. The work began. Raphael spent a year at the centre and some interesting work was achieved by the students before he left. Bridget stayed on and was loved by everybody.

Encouraged by the response, I went to suggest similar classes to a women's centre in Soho. How important it is to have the right person in charge! The character of an institution is moulded by the principal. This centre had a very different atmosphere. There was no proper administration or structure to the running of the place. Staff were nowhere to be found. It was dirty and the women were often drunk. There were fights, heartaches and no one seemed to care. At least they allowed us to work there. The first entertainment was at Christmas time. Rudi and Ray, two West Indian musicians who had a great understanding of human beings, agreed to play. I went along to see how the evening would turn out. They managed to provide entertainment and fun for the party, despite a happy lady pinching Rudi's bottom as he blew the saxophone. And Ray had to keep an eye on his belongings, which shifted from place to place. Again it was a pleasure to be with such warm people. They tended to let everything 'hang out', for there was nothing left to lose. Underneath the intoxication and frailty was a deep insight and a penetrating understanding of the world at large, which manifested itself in the odd pertinent remark. I hope that one day they can be settled in a more attractive centre. Despite the cynics, I do believe that most people appreciate and take care of surroundings which are clean and warm, both physically and morally.

The Christmas performance was followed up by Maria, an American girl, giving weekly drama therapy, and by Jaime, a South American artist whose skill was in using plasticine to make beautiful pictures. Jaime, who spoke little English at first, always came with Theresa, his wife. They showed the women how to use this simple technique. As with the wire sculpting, here was an easy technique that could be taught and provided a quick end result. This is important in circumstances where people are moving on. Kath and Mary gave toy making and leather work sessions at a men's prison with the same ease and success. These artists were exceptional in their maturity and down-to-earth understanding of life. The age of the tutor has little to do with the response to such workshops. A love of their craft, ease of communication, flexibility and an intuitive sensitivity to other people are the qualities needed for working in these areas. From my experience the young enjoy working with the elderly and the elderly with the young. Male inmates prefer to have a warm homely personality rather than a cover girl figure. Those suffering from social disability in the open community respond to personalities that almost border on 'characters', with strong energies. The last emotion any of these people require is pity. Concern yes, pity no.

One reason why the professional artist is so welcome to staff who care for such groups is that they recognise the value of 'an outside person', someone who is not wearing a uniform and whose skill has nothing to do with the environment into which he is coming. My admiration for those caring for the disabled is beyond description. It is so easy for us to breeze in and out, radiating good will, but to be able to do this through the endless problems and daily humdrum routine requires a special quality most of us do not possess. When remarking on this to someone, the reply is often, 'Yes, but then it is a vocation for them,' apparently dismissing it all as 'their' problem. Not nearly enough recognition and adequate material reward is given. Nor do I understand why those who care for the sick should be rewarded with a financial slap in the face.

By now we had evidence of the value of our work. In practically every case, after the three months free trial period was over, the sessions were taken over and continued by the individual institutions, many of whom applied to the education authorities for help.

Because of our non-administrative backgrounds Helen and I found it difficult to sit behind desks. Literally so. Helen would be in her chair interviewing someone; I would leave the room and return to find her perched on the radiator. My favourite place was the windowsill, as I have a fetish about fresh air, which in the winter did not endear me to my colleagues. Elizabeth, always serene, was the only one who remained seated behind her desk.

It was nearly Christmas again. The amount of work had doubled because of an ever-increasing demand for entertainment and creative classes. New regional services were developing. The backbone of the structure had been established and the hardest part was over. Helen felt it was time to move on towards her theatre work and to learn to slow down again.

After Christmas there was the good news that the Arts Council and DHSS had decided to show their approval by giving us small grants. To have the support of two government agencies from the opposite ends of our work was as it should be. The night before Helen left was a sleepless, panicky one for me. I realised that such a small project in terms of staff would always be, and rightly so, a stepping stone of experience for everyone except the organiser. It was a strange Friday when we said goodbye. Helen had become so much part of Shape. The next week a new colleague arrived, coming from a very different background in the commercial world. At first it was hard for her to understand the altruistic nature of the project. But after three months she was able to adjust and to adapt her considerable skills to Shape with great benefit.

This was the first year we were able to stand back and assess the overall picture of the work since Shape began. By far the greatest demand for activities and entertainment was coming from institutions for elderly people. I have visited and worked practically with movement in many different places for the elderly. This experience compels me to write down a few personal observations on some of the problems that they face when institutionalised. We all acknowledge (in a superficial way that prompts us to do nothing to alter the situation) that the breakdown of the family unit is the cause of much distress and unhappiness to the elderly. Once they lose the freedom of their own space, be it a poky little bedsitting room or as a member of a family, demoralisation sets in. Independence to choose when to eat, sleep and dress have gone.

So often I entered a ward where no one was talking to anyone else. I think in many ways this was an attempt to rebel and still be free, at least by rejecting those with whom the patients wished to speak. It was a gentle protest, probably the only choice left to them. Another reason may have been, as pointed out by a physiotherapist, that the older generation expects formal introductions, such as, 'This is Mr (or Mrs). . .'. It is not enough to say, 'Here is Betty who has come to join us.' Many wonderful old people assured me of their gratitude for the care they received. What was so hard for them to accept was the loss of dignity and their feeling of uselessness. The same story was told again and again: 'I was fine until I had to retire, then the trouble began.' This is a generation of people who were conditioned to feel fulfilled only through occupation and had little encouragement or time to learn to enjoy leisure.

Could there not be research work undertaken by the young, who relate to and understand the elderly so well? Perhaps this could be done through a Manpower Services scheme for the unemployed. For example, a start could be made by establishing what work there was within the institution with which the old people could help. Staff are always so hard pressed. There must be many tasks that could be done from a chair, such as rolling bandages, counting laundry, and so on. In America, the longstay patient is encouraged to have a small job and is financially rewarded for his services. I cannot imagine unions resenting such a scheme. Most of us, including union members, will look forward to the same problems in old age, unless room is made for a change. In America, a group of elderly people, tired of being referred to as senior citizens, geriatrics or whatever, formed themselves into a pressure group, 'The Grey Panthers'. This group pressed for anti-discrimination against elderly people. America is a country of professional consumers and therefore any pressure on public relations is an effective weapon. For example, no airline likes to have a bad press through refusing to accept passengers after a certain age, because they might drop dead on the plane. This was just one attitude the Grey Panthers were able to change. Unfortunately, organisations in this country seem to care little about their image and the service they give. There is a great deal of public prejudice against the disabled and elderly. However, one of the benefits of the International Year of Disabled People has been the efforts the media have taken to help the public become more aware and understanding about the rights and needs of the disabled. I should like to see more effort given towards encouraging the rest of us to ensure that the elderly are respected and end their days as dignified, independent human beings. The situation at present is quite the reverse. All the nursing care and attention does not compensate for the lack of contact with family and friends, and that is the responsibility of all of us. In addition, the media could help to re-educate the public to respect the elderly. The media could and should play a far greater part in encouraging us to have a sense of social responsibility towards each other, and especially those at a disadvantage.

The kind of activities Shape introduced went a little way towards making the old people's days more stimulating. There were the more accepted classes, such as painting or music. Then there was movement for the elderly, which is described in the second chapter of this book. Creative writing in a group was a way of telling each other about their past and present lives, of remembering experiences. When a student was not able to use the pen, her memories were spoken onto tapes. A newspaper of events happening in the hospital, and of ideas and suggestions, was written by the older patients. Even if a group consists of only two or three people it can be of tremendous value. For the very frail and elderly, young musicians sang and played the songs with which the old people grew up. This was much more useful than merely playing them a record. Here was an individual willing to teach them the words and melodies and thereby stimulate their memories.

In all creative work which artists introduce, it is particularly important to explain the reason for the activity. Never more so than in the case of older people. A bald opening statement, such as, 'Now we are going to hold an art class and do some painting', can make a person feel as if she is back at school. There will be a much better response if the class is introduced in this way: 'If you would like to paint today, please do join in; it can help to keep your fingers supple and maintaining concentration is a good discipline for the memory.' Maybe some will not hear or understand such an explanation, but others, who resent the loss of their dignity, will appreciate such words. Most older people are willing to try anything if they feel it helps towards their general well-being.

Terminal Hospitals
Our work here was probably monitored more carefully by the staff than in any other area. Rightly so, for it is essential that no added pressure or strain should be put on these students. Hospices are some of the most joyful institutions I have visited. Performers always like entertaining in these places. Folk, classical music, dance and poetry readings were the most frequently requested forms of entertainment. Regular weekly sessions were either visual art sessions or an actor reading extracts from favourite books. One artist began to paint a picture of the patients' choice. No one was well enough in this group to paint for himself; they lay in bed watching the picture grow, suggesting colours and design. Knowing that they would probably not see the finished result did not matter, for it was the pleasure of seeing something beginning that made them respond.

The artist can learn much from the experience of working with people close to death.

Psychiatric Hospitals

These audiences responded with vitality to every kind of performance or activity. Women's theatre groups, short plays with audience participation, mime, dance, folk, talks, any kind of music, were all welcomed wholeheartedly. There were two different kinds of audience within this heading. Firstly, there were those who were in a psychiatric unit of a general hospital and who in most instances would return to the mainstream of society. These audiences needed a different presentation from longterm patients, as they were often accustomed to going out for their entertainment and were therefore probably more selective. Yet it was often more difficult to perform here than at the long-stay psychiatric hospital. Short-term patients are more shocked at being in such a situation and at receiving a considerable amount of medication and intense treatment. This meant that audiences were less receptive. Because of this their willingness to participate in an after-event discussion used to surprise me at first; later I realised that all such discussions allowed a platform for their own problems to be touched upon by themselves in a very roundabout way. It was rather similar to prison inmates who liked learning to manipulate puppets. Through this medium they too found a way of expressing themselves, without having to identify personally, but through the character they had made.

For regular sessions for short-stay psychiatric patients, dance was always a favourite, with acting following closely behind. A mixture of the two is ideal. It is very important never to allow the students to feel inadequate, and a trust must be built up between tutor and students before sessions can be spontaneous and relaxed. Tension and trust are the qualities you hope to lose and find when working as a teacher. Many of the artists were disappointed at how few consultants and psychiatric staff knew about or came occasionally to look in on their work. It seemed always to be the occupational therapist or physiotherapist who took an interest. This was so with all the institutions. There was only the rare consultant who saw the potential of the artist in playing a healing role and watched closely the benefits it brought his patients. Mostly the work of artists was known about but still dismissed as purely 'diversional'.

We all need diversions, and all the more so when under pressure. One qualified beautician told me that she had offered her services free to a number of London hospitals. She thought some women who were well enough might enjoy having a massage or facial. Her offer was refused as impractical. Yet there is nothing more relaxing and good for the morale than having a facial or massage. Yoga classes, Tai Chi (a quiet slow form of Chinese movement designed to help people's well-being), meditation techniques, are often more effective and less harmful soothers than tranquillisers. Some enlightened hospitals recognise the value of using outside specialists as well as the usual medical team and I would hope that many more will soon follow their example.

Many times visitors came to ask what research projects were being done to measure our work. It annoyed a few people that we were not interested in such research. The reason for our attitude was that the work of the professional artist in these situations cannot be scientifically measured. It can only be assessed by the response of the students. That is all. How could it really be proved that Mrs X was more relaxed due to a drama session? There were so many factors that might have made Mrs X feel better that day. If you asked Mrs X, 'Did you feel more relaxed after that session?' she would reply truthfully, 'Yes'. That is probably the closest you would get to an evaluation. If people begin drawing graphs of behaviour patterns and moods based on responses, the artist will eventually lose the perspective with which he began his work. He will constantly be looking over his shoulder at the graph resulting from another artist's work and lose his own individual approach in order to try and achieve the same or better graph results. The artistic therapist, however, works with a different orientation. He is part of the medical team and therefore such scientific assessments may well be in his brief.

Long-stay psychiatric hospitals are an altogether different case from the short-term ones but they, too, badly need the stimulus of the arts. There are many people who were sent to these institutions because they have nowhere else to go, as was the case of the Polish refugees during the Second World War. There are others who are there because they are mentally ill and some who are just plain eccentric and not accepted by society. Whatever the reason, these people will probably remain in this environment. These institutions have little money allocated to them for entertainment and none at all for regular weekly sessions. Yet the apathy that surrounds such places cries out for any creative activities.

I should like to suggest that such places might consider allocating a workplace for the professional artist who often needs space but cannot afford it. Often in large institutions there are unused rooms. The artists, in return for the space, could involve interested residents in learning a craft or skill. The objects made could be sold outside, with the help of the artists, by residents who are well enough. This is not, however, the main purpose of the suggestion. There is a need for a complete reappraisal of life in long-stay institutions. At present they are one of the most neglected areas of our society. It would be interesting to begin by having one pilot scheme in a long-stay psychiatric hospital, whereby a group of artists, not necessarily of one discipline, worked for six months within the hospital on their own work, and at the same time became part of this community. They need not be resident, but this setting would be their professional workplace, where colleagues and friends would visit them. The residents in the hospital would be free to watch them work and hopefully get to know them. In this way it might be possible to establish a new kind of community with energy and vitality coming from outside. A similar scheme works successfully in France.

The words 'long stay' should be changed. I visited an institution which was called a home for 'incurables'. The residents were active people, but with that address on your letter it would be hard not to lose heart.

The only way Shape could take regular workshops into hospitals was by using artists on the Manpower Services schemes we had for unemployed people. They were paid for by the government. The weakness of using them here was that at the end of the allotted time the artist had to withdraw from an activity which might have just begun to build up. Nor were we allowed the freedom to choose exactly the right person for the work. Many of the artists were young, and inexperienced; taking them into such demanding situations could subject them to considerable strain. Nevertheless it was agreed by these hospitals and ourselves that something was better than nothing.

Once again it was dance that seemed to be such a wonderful outlet for these students of widely differing ages. Music was their favourite entertainment. You could have heard a pin drop in the audience when a jazz group played their contemporary sounds. Other performances ended up as a party, with some of the audience dancing in the aisles. Every style of social dance could be seen. Older people even managed to fit ballroom dancing to reggae music. Grey audiences were transformed, eyes became bright, faces alive, feet began tapping, hands clapped strenuously. Bands had to be sensitive to the risk of overstimulation. They had to use their intuition and to recognise when to change tempo and quieten the mood. Effects such as strobe lights were avoided because they tend to activate fits. Here were interesting, exciting, forgotten people with whom the artist could communicate and from whom he could learn.

Mentally handicapped institutions are probably the artists' favourite venue. These wonderful people receive with an enthusiasm that makes you glow. Those with Down's syndrome in particular have a sense of joy that I envy. There was a memorable moment at a Christmas party held at Normansfield Hospital, Teddington. Thinking I was really in the swing of things, I looked up to catch my partner gesticulating over my head to his friend as if to say (pointing his first finger to his head), 'she's crazy'. Abashed, I sat down and, quite properly, watched how to 'stay loose and dance properly'. Woolfgang had shown time and time again with his work amongst the mentally handicapped that their capabilities of independence and self-discipline are far underestimated. They may only have the intelligence of an eight year old child, yet inside there is a part of them which is adult or responds to adult treatment.

The Fourth Year
Many arts organisations were becoming more involved in these different pockets of the community. Fascinating projects and training courses were being run. Yet most of us were only

vaguely aware of each other's work. Shape organised a meeting. A pilot discussion on better ways of sharing information about our various activities was the topic of the afternoon seminar, but although many London-based arts organisations willingly attended, little change resulted. One happy outcome is that with the help of a London local radio station and telephone information line, news about arts opportunities and how to make use of all these groups is now readily available to the disadvantaged.

There were so many events that happened all at the same time in the fourth year, near Christmas as usual. We were given notice to leave Covent Garden; another regional service was being set up; we were in the middle of organising our first variety performance for the handicapped. Where to begin unravelling the tangled threads was a problem. At the same time there were a number of press interviews because of the forthcoming variety concert. One or our difficulties had always been Shape's success. People tended to imagine that this project, which covered such a wide area and organised the development of regional services, must be run by a large staff. Journalists who came to the office looked stunned when they saw three of us. 'Is this all of you?' 'Yes,' we said apologetically. 'But we have more than 500 artists on our register,' we added, hoping that this would make up for their disappointment.

The priority was the Christmas show. The variety concert was the beginning of a focus which all the previous work had built towards. The title of the show explained all: 'Time To Get Out'. To see isolated people encouraged to come out of their surroundings and be entertained in public places like the rest of society was the wish of us all. Our American counterpart, Hospital Artists Inc., had for a long time operated a scheme whereby many Broadway theatres papered the house by donating tickets to HAI. With a large system of voluntary help, they offered the tickets daily to a network of institutions. Our show was just a start. Today Shape has a ticket subsidy scheme, and many people are making use of this service and getting out to entertainments.

There were difficulties in organising such an event. Most performers were willing to take part for love on the day, but were not able to spare the time for a rehearsal beforehand.

Planning a programme and timing it, as well as meeting all the lighting requirements and needs of the artists by remote control, was a headache. The Commonwealth Institute offered us their theatre for a very reduced fee. Interaction Trust volunteered a director on the day.

I thought that the problems of finding transport and volunteer staff might make hospitals reticent about coming. The thought could not have been more misplaced. Long-stay psychiatric hospitals from as far away as Suffolk were prepared to make the journey. The response was overwhelming and our only problem was in having to limit the numbers. We all became very excited. There was a large volunteer team of artists who organised themselves to serve behind the bar, carry wheelchairs, help people go to the lavatories, welcome them at the main door, and generally to be on hand. The morning of the show arrived. The steel band from Huntercombe Borstal was the first to arrive. Brian Rix, who had agreed to compere, was next. He looked a little alarmed that most of the performers were not yet there. Eventually the whole cast arrived. It was chaos. The magician complained that someone had touched his table; different groups' sound effects and endless wires got tangled up; dancers needed a long limber-up; we had only two hours to run through. Everyone wondered if it would ever be put together.

The audience began to arrive while the rehearsal was still going on. Had we known that hospitals were bringing mostly older patients we would have planned a different programme. That was our first mistake. It took an hour to seat everyone and I realised with dismay that it would not be possible to allow the wheelchairs to come out at the interval, as it would take too long to reseat them. That was our second mistake. The show began. It was incredible to see such a form to it after the disastrous morning. The performers were superb: Ballet Rambert, musicians, Maas Movers, reggae steel bands, music hall, magic. Our third mistake was that the loud amplification of most bands was too much for the older people. Yet despite all this the letters of appreciation poured in afterwards. We were a little hurt when *Stage* reviewed the show somewhat coolly as if it had been a West End production. It was a first attempt, basically organised by three people who had no theatre direction experience. The admission was free and all expenses were paid out of our fund-raising efforts. In future I hope that a West End management would offer to put on a show, for the quality should be of the best for such audiences.

One of the most successful spots had been the Borstal Boys' steel band. Since then they have been requested to perform at a number of hospitals.

Christmas passed. The show was behind us and the work went on. A new office was found, two tiny attic rooms overlooking the chimney pots of London. At last we became a registered charity in our own right. A committee was formed. Shape became respectable. Packing up at Covent Garden I realised that it was the right time to move both the office and myself. Everything I had set out to do had begun. The idea was established. The service could and should be run by a new team. I thought the next step after all these previous experiences was to establish an international information exchange network that could provide details of arts opportunities for disadvantaged people within many countries, as well as encouraging a sharing of new ideas. It was a now-or-never decision to leave. The answer was now to begin again.

ARTS ORGANISATIONS YOU CAN GET IN TOUCH WITH

Arts Councils

Arts Council of Great Britain — 105 Piccadilly, London W1V 0AU
01-629 9495

Arts Council of Northern Ireland — 181a Stranmillis Road, Belfast BT9 5DU
0232 663591

Scottish Arts Council — 19 Charlotte Square, Edinburgh EH2 4DF
031-226 6051

Welsh Arts Council — Holst House, 9 Museum Place, Cardiff CF1 3NX
0222 394711

Regional Arts Associations

East Midlands Arts Association — Mountfields House, Forest Road, Loughborough, Leicestershire LE11 3HU
0509 218292

Eastern Arts Association — 8/9 Bridge Street, Cambridge
0223 67707

Greater London Arts Association — 25-31 Tavistock Place, London WC1H 9SF
01-388 2211

Lincolnshire and Humberside Arts — Saint Hugh's, Newport, Lincoln LN1 3DN
0522 33555

Merseyside Arts Association	Bluecoat Chambers, School Lane, Liverpool L1 3BX 051-709 0671/2/3
Northern Arts	10 Osborne Terrace, Newcastle-upon-Tyne NE2 1NZ 0632 816334
North West Arts	12 Harter Street, Manchester M1 6HY 061-228 3062
South East Arts Association	9/10 Crescent Road, Tunbridge Wells, Kent TN2 2LU 0892 41666
Southern Arts Association	19 Southgate Street, Winchester, Hampshire SO23 7EB 0962 55099
South West Arts	23 Southernhay East, Exeter, Devon EX1 1QL 0392 38924
West Midlands Arts	Lloyds Bank Chambers, Market Street, Stafford ST16 2AP 0785 59231
Yorkshire Arts Association	Glyde House, Glydegate, Bradford, West Yorkshire BD5 0BQ 0274 23051
South East Wales Arts Association	Victoria Street, Cwmbran, Gwent NP44 3JP

Arts Organisations

Action Space	The Drill Hall, 16 Chenies Street, London WC1 01-637 7664
Association of Dance Therapists	7 Ashlake Road, Streatham, London SW16
British Association of Art Therapists	13c Northwood Road, London N6 5TL
British Association of Drama Therapists	7 Hatfield Road, St Albans, Herts.

British Society for Music Therapy	48 Lancaster Road, London N6 01-883 1331
British Institute for the Study of the Arts in Therapy (and Sesame)	Christchurch, 27 Blackfriars Road, London SE1 8NY 01-633 9690
British Library of Tape Recordings for Hospital Patients	12 Lant Street, London SE1 1QR 01-407 9417
British Theatre Association	9 Fitzroy Square, London W1P 6AE 01-387 2666
Calibre-Cassette Library for the Blind and Handicapped	Aylesbury, Bucks HP20 1HU 0296 32339
Central Bureau for Educational Visits and Exchanges	43 Dorset Street, London W1H 3FN 01-486 5101 *and* 3 Bruntsfield Crescent, Edinburgh EH10 4HD 031-447 8024
Cockpit Theatre and Arts Workshop	Gateforth Street, Marylebone, London NW1 01-262 7907
Council for Music in Hospitals	340 Lower Road, Little Bookham, Surrey KT23 4RE
The Dance Drama Theatre	1 The Warren, Carshalton Beeches, Surrey SM5 4EQ 01-643 4833
Drama with the Blind	Advisory Group, c/o Royal National Institute for the Blind, 224/8 Great Portland Street, London S1N 6AA 01-388 1266
The Drama Board and Central Council for Amateur Theatre	PO Box 44, Banbury, Oxon OX15 4EQ 0295 50860

East Midlands Shape	New Farm, Walton by Kimcote, Nr Lutterworth, Leics. LE11 3HU 045-55 3882
Educational Drama Association	Drama Centre, Reaside School, Rea St South, Birmingham B5 6LB 021-622 3107
Inter-Action Trust	Talacre Open Space, 15 Wilkin Street, London NW5 01-485 0881
Interim Theatre Company Ltd (Deaf-Hearing Company)	3 Spring Lane, London SE25 4SP 01-656 9653
Interlink	358 Strand, London WC2R 0HS 01-836 2204/836 5819

(An international information network on arts opportunities for disabled and disadvantaged people)

Ludus Dance in Education	Rhodes House, 114 St Leonardgate, Lancaster LA1 1NN 0524 67728
National Association for Drama in Education and Children's Theatre National Council of Theatre for Young People	British Theatre Centre, 9 Fitzroy Square, London W1P 6AE 01-387 2666
Natural Dance Theatre	The Natural Dance Workshop, Playspace, Peto Place, London NW1 4DT 01-935 1410
Neighbourhood Open Workshops	2-4 University Road, Belfast BT7 1NT 0232 42910
Nordhoff Music Therapy Centre	c/o Goldie Leigh Hospital, Lodge Hill, Abbey Wood, London SE2 0AY
Puppet Centre – Educational Puppetry Association	c/o Battersea Arts Centre, Lavender Hill, London SW11 5TJ 01-223 5356

Scottish Mime Theatre	36a Lavriston Place, Edinburgh EH3 9EZ 031-229 2821
Shape	7 Fitzroy Square, London W1P 6AE 01-338 9622
Shape up North	The Belle Vue Centre, Belle Vue Road, Leeds LS3 1HG 0532 31005
Standing Conference for Amateur Music	26 Bedford Square, London WC1B 3HU 01-636 4066
Scottish Amateur Music Association	7 Randolph Crescent, Edinburgh EH3 7TH
Scottish Committee for Arts and Disability	18/19 Claremont Crescent, Edinburgh EH7 4QD 031-556 3882
South West Shape	c/o South West Arts, 23 Southernhay East, Exeter, Devon EX1 1QL 0392 38924
Tibble Trust (Music for the Elderly)	36 Belsize Court, Wedderburn, London NW3 5QJ
Welsh Committee	c/o South East Wales Arts Association, Victoria Street, Cwmbran, Gwent NP44 3JP 06333 67530
The Workshop	34 Hamilton Place, Edinburgh EH3 5AX 031-225 7942

Organisations that run courses in movement or drama

Hertfordshire College of Art and Design	Hatfield Road, St Albans, Herts. AL1 3RS
British Association of Dramatherapy	72 Hillmorton Road, Rugby, Warwicks
Sesame (Drama and Dance in Therapy)	Christchurch, 27 Blackfriars Road, London SE1 8NY

Dance in Special Education,
Laban Centre for Movement and
   Dance,
Gina Levete, Interlink

University of London
Goldsmith's College
New Cross, London SE14 6NW
358 The Strand, London WC2

SUGGESTED BOOKS

The first four books, although not written with disabled students in mind, are full of ideas, some of which can be adapted.

Improvisation for the Theatre, Viola Spolin; Pitmans.

Theatre Movement. The Actor and his Space, Nancy King; Drama Book Specialists, NY.

Dance: Elementary Education, Ruth Lovell Murray; Harper & Row.

The Mastery of Movement, McDonald and Evans.

The Mime Book, Claude Kipins; Harper Colophon Books.

Motives for Mime, Pat Keyell; Evans.

To Move, To Learn, Kate Witkin; Schocken Books, NY.

One Hundred Plus Ideas for Drama, Anna Scher and Charles Verral; Heinemann Educational Books.

Creative Therapy, Sue Jennings, ed; Pitmans.

Remedial Drama, Sue Jennings; Pitmans.

Physical and Creative Activities for Handicapped Children, C. Upton, ed; Cambridge University Press.

Drama as a Learning Medium, Dorothy Heathcote and Betty Jane Wagner; Hutchinson.

Game-Songs Handbook, Harriet Powell, ed Ed Berman, Interaction Impress.

British Alternative Theatre Directory, John Offord Publications Ltd., PO Box 64, Eastbourne BN21 3LW.

Directory of Arts Centres 2, John Offord Publications Ltd.

Children's World of Art (directory of children's arts activities), Central Bureau of Educational Visits and Exchanges, Seymour Mews House, Seymour Mews, London W1

Puppetry for Mentally Handicapped People, Caroline Astell-Burt; Souvenir Press.

Art Activities for the Handicapped, Sally M. Atack; Souvenir Press.

A reading list of Arts and the Handicapped (Reference Sheet 7) is available free from the Information Section of the Arts Council of Great Britain, which will also provide a list of colleges where dance can be part of a course, and a list of dance schools.